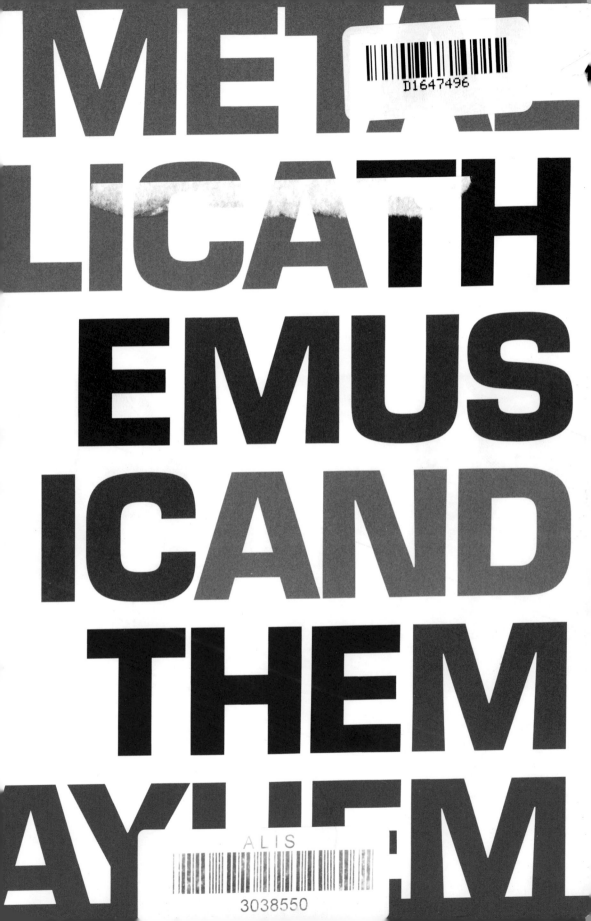

Copyright © 1995 Omnibus Press
This edition © 2010 Omnibus Press
(A Division of Music Sales Limited)

Cover & book designed by Fresh Lemon
Picture research by Jacqui Black

ISBN: 978.1.84938.662.3
Order No: OP53834

Exclusive Distributors
Music Sales Limited, 14/15 Berners Street, London,
W1T 3LJ.

Music Sales Corporation,
257 Park Avenue South, New York, NY 10010, USA.

Macmillan Distribution Services,
56 Parkwest Drive, Derrimut, Vic 3030, Australia.

Picture credits:
All pictures courtesy of LFI.
Except p16 Ebet Roberts/Referns; p27 Mick Hutson /
Redferns; p55 Paul Natkin/WireImage; p56 Pete Cronin /
Redferns; p106 Clay Mclachlan/Getty Images.

Colour section:
All pictures courtesy of LFI.
p1 WENN, Ekstra Bladet; p2 WENN; p4 Getty;
p6 Neal Preston/CORBIS; p7 Redferns / Mick Hutson;
p8 Neal Preston/CORBIS, Jeff Kravitz/FilmMagic

Every effort has been made to trace the copyright
holders of the photographs in this book but one or
two were unreachable. We would be grateful if the
photographers concerned would contact us.

Printed in the E.U.

A catalogue record for this book is available from the
British Library.
Visit Omnibus Press on the web at www.omnibuspress.com

METALLICA
THE MUSIC AND THE MAYHEM
MALCOLM DOME AND MICK WALL

OMNIBUS PRESS

LONDON / NEW YORK / PARIS / SYDNEY / COPENHAGEN / BERLIN / MADRID / TOKYO

1962
FEBRUARY 10
Cliff Burton born in Castro Valley, California.

1962
NOVEMBER 18
Kirk Hammett born in San Francisco, California.

1972
James begins piano lessons.

1973
FEBRUARY
Lars sees Deep Purple with his father Torben in Copenhagen. It is his first rock concert.

1963
AUGUST 3
James Hetfield born in Downey, California.

1964
OCTOBER 23
Rob Trujillo born in Santa Monica, California.

1963
MARCH 4
Jason Newsted born in Battle Creek, Michigan.

1963
DECEMBER 26
Lars Ulrich born in Gentofte, Demark.

1975

After a spell learning piano, Cliff takes up bass guitar. Lars also receives his first drum kit.

1977
SEPTEMBER

James starts high school in Downey, where he meets Ron McGovney.

1978

James joins his first band, Obsession, with Jim Arnold, Rich and Ron Veloz.

1980

James forms a new band, Phantom Lord, with Hugh Tanner and Jim Mulligan. After taking up guitar, Kirk forms his first real band, Exodus, with vocalist Paul Baloff and fellow guitarist, Gary Holt. In Castro Valley, Cliff is winding down his first band, EZ Street, before forming Agents Of Misfortune.

1979

James' mother, Cynthia, dies from cancer. He leaves Obsession after moving to La Brea, California.

1977

James drops piano in favour of guitar. Jason forms his first band, Diamond, in Niles, Michigan only for his family to relocate to Kalamazoo months later.

1981

Now resident in San Francisco, Lars makes a pilgrimage from the USA to London, England to see his favourite band, Diamond Head. He befriends them, and even stays at the house of guitarist Brian Tatler for several weeks before returning home to the States.

1981
MAY 9

James and Lars meet for the first time at Newport Beach, California.

1981
JUNE

Ron McGovney joins James in Phantom Lord, who rename themselves Leather Charm. However, the new line up soon falls apart.

1982
MARCH 14

Metallica play their first concert at Radio City, Anaheim, California with new bassist, Ron McGovney.

1981
OCTOBER 15

Lars and James form Metallica. Lead guitarist Dave Mustaine soon joins them after responding to an advertisement in *The Recycler* newspaper. They make Los Angeles their temporary home.

1982
APRIL

Metallica record the 'Power Metal' demo featuring 'Hit The Lights', 'Motorbreath', 'The Mechanix' and 'Jump In The Fire'.

1981
OCTOBER 31

Jason moves to Phoenix, Arizona where he joins a local band, Dredlox. After various line up changes, the band will become Dogz, then Flotsam and Jetsam.

1982
MARCH

Metallica record new demos: another version of 'Hit The Lights' and two covers, 'Killing Time' and 'Let It Loose'.

1982
JANUARY

First original Metallica song, 'Hit The Lights', is recorded.

1982
JUNE 14

'Hit The Lights' appears on the *Metal Massacre* compilation LP. The band is incorrectly listed as 'Mettallica' on the sleeve.

1982
NOVEMBER 29

After opening for power metal act Y&T in Los Angeles, Metallica headline their first show in San Francisco. Kirk Hammett's group, Exodus, provide support.

1983
FEBRUARY 11

On Cliff's recommendation, Metallica move their base of operations from Los Angeles to San Francisco.

1982
JULY 6

Metallica record seven song 'No Life Till Leather' demo.

1982
DECEMBER 28

Having seen bassist Cliff Burton onstage with his latest band, Trauma, at Los Angeles club Whisky a Go Go, Hetfield and Ulrich ask him to join Metallica. After some consideration, Cliff agrees.

1982
NOVEMBER 30

Metallica play their last gig with bassist Ron McGovney. He leaves the group 10 days later.

1982
APRIL 23

Metallica play their first and only gig as a five piece when Damien Phillips (aka Jeff Warner) joins the group on guitar, thus freeing up James to concentrate on vocals. After an alleged spat with Dave Mustaine, Phillips quickly exits the band. Hetfield now consolidates his position as singer/rhythm guitarist.

1983
MARCH 5

Cliff makes his debut appearance with Metallica at The Stone Club in San Francisco. Again, Kirk Hammett's band Exodus provides support.

1983
MAY 3

Metallica sign a deal with
Megaforce Records.

1983
APRIL 16

Kirk makes his debut
appearance with Metallica
at a concert in Dover,
New Jersey.

1983
JULY 16

Kill 'Em All is released. The record
will sell over three million units in
the next decade. Two singles from
Kill 'Em All, 'Whiplash' and 'Jump
In The Fire', are also released.

1983
APRIL 1

After continuing personality
clashes with Dave
Mustaine, Lars, James
and Cliff ask Kirk to join
Metallica. Mustaine plays
his last gig with the band
nine days later.

1984
FEBRUARY 3

Following the release of 'Jump In
The Fire' as a single in Europe on
January 20, Metallica begin their first
European tour alongside death metal
band Venom in Zurich, Switzerland.

1983
MAY 10

The band begin recording sessions
for their debut album, *Metal Up Your
Ass*, in Rochester, New York. After
concerns over the album's name, it is
rechristened *Kill 'Em All*.

1983
SEPTEMBER 24

Metallica start work on a new
set of demos.

1983
JULY 27

Metallica begin a two month US tour, 'Kill 'Em All For
One', with British metal group Raven in support.

1984
SEPTEMBER 12

Metallica sign a new record deal with Elektra Records, who re-release *Ride The Lightning* on 16 November. It will go on to sell over five million copies by 2003.

1984
NOVEMBER 18

Metallica begin their first major European tour. It concludes with a headlining appearance at London's Lyceum club on 20 December.

1984
FEBRUARY 20

Metallica start recording their second album, *Ride The Lightning,* at Copenhagen's Sweet Silence Studios.

1985
JANUARY 19

Metallica start their first co-headlining tour of the States with WASP in Nova Scotia.

1984
MARCH 26

Metallica make their first appearance at London's legendary Marquee Club. Their second European tour will commence two months later.

1984
AUGUST 1

Metallica have their first meeting with Cliff Burnstein of Q Prime, who, alongside Peter Mensch, will become their co-manager. A day later, the band are released from their contract with Megaforce Records by owner John Zazula.

1984
JULY 27

Ride The Lightning is released. It spawns three singles: 'Fade To Black', 'Creeping Death' and 'For Whom The Bell Tolls'.

1985
AUGUST 17

Metallica make their debut at the fifth annual 'Monsters Of Rock' festival at Castle Donington, England alongside Ratt and Bon Jovi.

1985
MARCH 6

Flotsam And Jetsam's Jason Newsted attends Metallica's gig in Phoenix, Arizona. He has a front row ticket.

1985
MARCH 9

Ride The Lightning reaches number 100 in the US charts and number 87 in the UK. Metallica celebrate the news by getting very drunk. They conclude their US tour nine days later.

1985
DECEMBER 27

Metallica finally finish recording *Master Of Puppets.*

1986
MARCH 27

Metallica begin their 'Damage Inc.' tour of the US in Wichita, Kansas supporting Ozzy Osbourne. It will be their last tour as a support act.

1986
MARCH 3

Master Of Puppets is released in the States. The album becomes Metallica's first gold record, spending 72 weeks in the charts, and peaking at number 29. (It reached number 41 in the UK.) *Master Of Puppets* will go on to sell over six million copies in the States alone. Three US singles are released from the album: the title track, 'Battery' and '(Welcome Home) Sanatorium'.

1985
SEPTEMBER 1

Metallica begin recording their third album, *Master Of Puppets,* again at Copenhagen's Sweet Silence Studios. Fleming Rasmussen produces.

1985
SEPTEMBER 30

In a break from studio duties, Metallica appear at Oakland's 'Day On The Green' Festival, playing to over 60,000 fans.

1986
SEPTEMBER 10

The 'Damage Inc.' tour arrives in Europe with a date in Cardiff, Wales. Eleven days later, Metallica make their first headlining appearance at London's Hammersmith Odeon.

1987
MARCH 23

James manages to break his arm for a second time while skateboarding in an empty swimming pool. Metallica cancel a scheduled appearance on US comedy show *Saturday Night Live* while he recovers.

1986
JULY 16

James breaks his arm while skateboarding in Indiana. Metallica's guitar technician, John Marshall, takes up onstage duties as rhythm guitarist while a heavily bandaged James temporarily becomes lead vocalist.

1986
OCTOBER 7

Cliff's funeral takes place in Castro Valley, California. His ashes are scattered at Maxwell Ranch.

1987
FEBRUARY 8

Metallica's worldwide 'Damage Inc.' tour finally comes to a close in Zwolle, Holland.

1986
SEPTEMBER 27

While en route from Stockholm to Copenhagen, Metallica's tour bus crashes. Cliff Burton is killed in the accident.

1986
OCTOBER 31

Following his last gig with Flotsam And Jetsam, Jason Newsted is confirmed as Metallica's new bassist.

1986
NOVEMBER 8

Jason makes his live debut with Metallica at the Country Club in Reseda, California. The band then fly to Japan for a short tour, before returning to the US and Canada for more dates.

1987
AUGUST 21

Metallica's new covers EP, *Garage Days Revisited,* arrives in shops. An 'unofficial' release, it still manages to break into the US and UK charts at number 28 and number 27 respectively. Jason is credited as 'Jason Newkid' in the sleeve notes.

1987
DECEMBER 4

As a tribute to their late bassist, Metallica release *Cliff 'Em All,* a video collection capturing amateur footage of Cliff with the band dating from 1983-86. It will sell over three million copies.

1988
JANUARY 29

Metallica again venture to Los Angeles to begin work on their next album, *...And Justice For All.*

1987
AUGUST 20

Metallica play a secret warm-up gig at London's 100 Club before their second appearance at Castle Donington's 'Monsters Of Rock' festival two days later.

1988
MAY 27

Metallica join Scorpions, Dokken and Van Halen on the 'Monsters Of Rock' US tour, playing to crowds of over 50,000. While on the road, *Master Of Puppets* reaches platinum status with over one million copies sold.

1988
SEPTEMBER 3

The single 'Harvester Of Sorrows' reaches number 20 in the UK charts.

1987
NOVEMBER 5

Confirming their new popularity, Metallica's second album, *Ride The Lightning,* is certified gold in the US. *Garage Days Revisited* is soon awarded the same status.

1988
SEPTEMBER 6

...And Justice For All is released. Despite its curious production values, the album reaches number six in the US charts, going on to sell over eight million units. When released in the UK in September, the record peaks at number four.

1988
SEPTEMBER 11

The European leg of the 'Damaged Justice' tour begins in Budapest, Hungary. The tour will reach the States by 15 November, with Queensrÿche in support.

1989
JANUARY 9

'One' is released as a single in the US. It is Metallica's first Top 40 hit there, peaking at number 35. When released in the UK three months later, 'One' reaches number 13.

1989
OCTOBER 8

Metallica conclude their 'Damaged Justice' tour in San Paulo, Brazil.

1988
DECEMBER 6

Metallica begin filming their first ever promotional video for the track 'One'. The finished clip features footage from the cult anti-war film *Johnny Got His Gun*.

1990
JANUARY

Metallica record a cover version of Queen's 'Stone Cold Crazy' for inclusion on Elektra's 40th anniversary collection, *Rubaiyat*.

1989

After playing in several local bands, Rob Trujillo joins Suicidal Tendencies on bass guitar.

1989
MAY 1

After comprehensively touring the US, Metallica begin their world tour with a gig in Auckland, New Zealand.

1989
FEBRUARY 22

Metallica perform 'One' at the Grammy Awards, where *...And Justice For All* is nominated in the 'Best Metal Album' category. They lose to Jethro Tull. Subsequent record covers for *...And Justice For All* bear the sticker 'Grammy Award Losers'.

1990
FEBRUARY 22

A year after losing out to Jethro Tull, Metallica win their first Grammy for 'One' in 'Best Metal Performance'.

1991
JULY 30

The video for Metallica's new single 'Enter Sandman' premieres on MTV. 'Enter Sandman' reaches number five and number 16 in the UK and US charts.

1990
AUGUST 13

James and Lars begin recording rough demos for the next Metallica album.

1990
OCTOBER 6

Metallica begin recording their fifth album at One On One Studios in California with new producer, Bob Rock.

1990
NOVEMBER 9

Lars, James and Kirk play at a *Rip* magazine party, held in the Hollywood Palladium. They are joined onstage by Guns N' Roses' Axl Rose, Slash and Duff McKagan. Skid Row's Sebastian Bach also takes to the stage, singing 'Whiplash'.

1991
FEBRUARY 22

Metallica win 'Best Metal Performance' for their cover of 'Stone Cold Crazy' at the Grammys. Rob Trujillo's band, Suicidal Tendencies, are also nominated in the same category.

1990
MAY

Metallica appear at several European festivals, while also playing another low key date at London's Marquee Club.

1991
APRIL – JULY

Finishing touches are made to Metallica's new album at Vancouver's Little Rock Studios and A&M Studios in Hollywood. The album is completed on 10 July.

1991
AUGUST 17

Metallica make their third appearance at Castle Donington's 'Monsters Of Rock' festival. Six weeks later, they perform at Moscow's Tushino Airfield with AC/DC and Pantera.

1992
FEBRUARY 25

Metallica play 'Enter Sandman' at the Grammy Awards, where they win 'Best Metal Performance' for *The Black Album*.

1992
AUGUST 8

During a show at the Olympic Stadium in Montreal, Canada, James suffers second and third degree burns to his face, hands, arms and legs when he accidentally strays into a pyrotechnic flame display during 'Fade To Black'.

1992
APRIL 20

Metallica play a three song set at The Freddie Mercury Tribute Concert, held in London's Wembley Stadium. James also performs a version of 'Stone Cold Crazy' with Queen and Black Sabbath's Tony Iommi.

1991
OCTOBER 12

The 'Wherever I May Roam' world tour officially begins.

1991
AUGUST 12

Metallica's new self-titled record is released. It becomes known as *The Black Album*. Debuting at number one in both the UK and US charts, it will spawn five hit singles and sell over 22 million copies worldwide.

1992
JULY 17

Metallica begin a 24-date co-headlining US tour with Guns N' Roses.

1992
NOVEMBER 17

The band release *A Year And A Half In The Life Of Metallica (Parts I And II)* on video.

1994
JULY 3

Rob Trujillo and Suicidal Tendencies join Metallica onstage for a cover of Anti-Nowhere League's 'So What?'

1993
JANUARY 22

Metallica start their 'Nowhere Else To Roam' tour which takes them to Singapore, Thailand and Indonesia, among other countries.

1993
JULY 4

After two years on the road, Metallica play the final date of their tour at Werchter, Belgium.

1993
NOVEMBER 23

Metallica release a three-CD, three-video box set collection called *Live Shit: Binge & Purge*.

1992
SEPTEMBER 10

Metallica win 'Best Heavy Metal/Hard Rock Video' for 'Enter Sandman' at the *MTV Music Awards*.

1994
MAY 30

Metallica begin their 'Shit Hits The Sheds: Binging And Purging Across The USA' tour with Danzig and Suicidal Tendencies providing support.

1995
MAY

Metallica begin recording
sessions for their new album
with producer Bob Rock.

1996
FEBRUARY

Metallica finish work on their
sixth studio album at The Plant
Studios in Sausalito, California.

1995
AUGUST 26

Metallica again appear at
Castle Donington's 'Monsters
Of Rock' festival.

1995
SEPTEMBER 3

Metallica appear at the 'Polar
Beach Party' in Tuktoyaktuk, deep
within the Canadian tundra. Hole
and Veruca Salt offer support.

1995
AUGUST 23

Metallica play a 'members
only' concert for fans at
London's Astoria Two.

1995
DECEMBER 14

Billed as The Lemmys, Metallica
play a set of seven Motörhead
covers at the Whisky A Go-Go
on the occasion of Lemmy's
50th birthday.

1994
AUGUST 21

On the final date of the tour, Judas
Priest singer Rob Halford joins Metallica
onstage in Miami to perform a cover
version of Priest's own 'Rapid Fire'.

1996
MAY 21

Metallica release a new single, 'Until
It Sleeps'. It reaches number five and
number 10 in the UK and US charts.

1996
AUGUST 4

At the last 'Lollapalooza' show, Metallica are joined onstage by Lemmy and Alice In Chains' Jerry Cantrell. They perform renditions of Motörhead's 'Overkill' and 'For Whom The Bell Tolls'.

1996
SEPTEMBER 6

Metallica begin the European leg of 'Poor Touring Me' in Vienna, Austria.

1997
JANUARY 26

Lars marries his girlfriend, Skylar, at a ceremony in Las Vegas.

1996
NOVEMBER 16

Though scheduled to play 'King Nothing', Metallica switch tracks at the last minute and perform the expletive ridden 'So What?' instead at the *MTV Europe Music Awards*.

1996
JUNE 3

Metallica's new album, *Load,* is released. It debuts at number one in the UK and US charts, spawns six singles and sells over seven million copies worldwide.

1996
SEPTEMBER 4

Metallica perform 'Until It Sleeps' at the *MTV Music Awards*.

1996
JUNE 27

Metallica tour as part of the 'Lollapalooza' festival. They are supported by Soundgarden and Rancid.

1996
DECEMBER 19

Metallica begin the US leg of their 'Poor Touring Me' tour in Fresno, California.

1997
AUGUST 17
James marries his girlfriend, Francesca.

1997
NOVEMBER 11
To mark the release of a new single, 'The Memory Remains', Metallica play a free concert at CoreStates Arena in Philadelphia. 'The Memory Remains' reaches number 13 and number 28 in the UK and US charts.

1997
OCTOBER
Metallica finish work on their new record.

1997
MAY 28
'Poor Touring Me' dates end in Edmonton, Canada.

1997
AUGUST 22-24
Metallica appear at Belgium's 'Pukkelpop', Germany's 'Blind Man's Ball' and England's 'Reading Festival'.

1997
JULY
Metallica enter the studio to begin work on a new album.

1997
OCTOBER 18
Metallica perform their first ever acoustic show at Neil Young's 'Bridge School' benefit concert. Alice In Chains' Jerry Cantrell joins the band onstage for a version of Lynyrd Skynyrd's 'Tuesday's Gone'.

1997
JANUARY 27
Metallica perform 'King Nothing' at the *American Music Awards,* where they win 'Best Metal/Hard Rock Album'.

1997
NOVEMBER 17

Metallica's new album, *Re-Load,* is released. It produces three hit singles – 'The Memory Remains', 'The Unforgiven II' and 'Fuel' – and sells over three million copies.

1997
DECEMBER 8

Metallica win 'Best Hard Rock' act at the *Billboard Awards.*

1998
JUNE 13

James' daughter, Cali Tee Hetfield, is born.

1998
MARCH 22

Lars' mother, Lone, passes away.

1997
DECEMBER 6

Metallica perform 'The Memory Remains' alongside guest vocalist Marianne Faithfull on *Saturday Night Live.*

1998
JANUARY 31

Kirk marries girlfriend Lani in a ceremony in Hawaii.

1998
JUNE 24

American shows for 'Poor Re-Touring Me' start in Palm Beach, Florida.

1998
APRIL 2

'Poor Re-Touring Me' shows begin in Newcastle, Australia.

METALLICA TIMELINE • METALLICA TIMELINE

1998
AUGUST 15

Jason joins Sepultura onstage in Brazil.

1998
NOVEMBER 6

While in London on a promotional tour, Kirk is rushed to hospital for an emergency appendectomy.

1999
FEBRUARY 24

Metallica win 'Best Metal Performance' for 'Better Than You' at the Grammys.

1998
SEPTEMBER 15

Metallica return to the studio to cut several new cover versions for a forthcoming release.

1998
OCTOBER 18

Metallica join Hugh Hefner at the Playboy Mansion, where the band plays a short set.

1998
AUGUST 5

Lars' son, Myles, is born.

1998
NOVEMBER 23

Garage Inc., an amalgamation of Metallica's previous *Garage Days* EP, various B-sides and new cover versions, is released. It goes to number two and number four in the US and UK charts, and spawns four singles.

1998
SEPTEMBER 13

'Poor Re-Touring Me' shows conclude in San Diego, California.

1998
DECEMBER 8

Metallica release *Cunning Stunts,* a 175-minute concert film on DVD.

1999
APRIL 21-22

Metallica join conductor Michael Kamen and the San Francisco Symphony Orchestra in Berkeley, California to tape their *S&M* shows.

1999
APRIL 12

Metallica begin another tour, this time christened 'The Garage Remains The Same', in Hawaii.

1999
DECEMBER 31

Metallica perform a New Year's Eve/ New Millennium show with Ted Nugent and Kid Rock in Pontiac, Michigan.

1999
NOVEMBER 22

The *S&M* live symphonic album is released. It reaches number two and number 33 in the US and UK charts and spawns three singles.

1999
APRIL 7

Joining past winners who include Carlos Santana, Janis Joplin and John Lee Hooker, Metallica are awarded their very own 'Walk Of Fame' plaque at the Bay Area Music Awards.

1999
JULY 24

Metallica appear at 'Woodstock II'.

2000
FEBRUARY 23

Metallica win another 'Best Metal Performance' Grammy for their cover of Thin Lizzy's 'Whiskey In The Jar'.

1999
NOVEMBER 19-23

Metallica play two further *S&M* symphonic shows in Berlin, Germany and Madison Square Garden, New York.

2000
APRIL 8

Metallica and Michael Kamen receive the Arthur M. Sochot Award for Excellence for their collaboration on *S&M*.

2001
FEBRUARY 21

Despite competition from guitarists Peter Frampton and Joe Satriani, Metallica win a Grammy for 'Best Hard Rock Instrumental Performance' for 'The Call Of Ktulu'.

2000
NOVEMBER 30

Metallica perform at the *VH1 My Music Awards.* They win 'Gods Of Thunder' and 'Best Stage Spectacle' awards. It will be Jason's last appearance with the band.

2000
JUNE 20

The *S&M* live DVD is released. On the same day, Metallica begin their 'Summer Sanatorium' tour with Korn, Kid Rock and System Of A Down offering support.

2001
JANUARY 17

Jason announces he is leaving Metallica.

2000
MAY 9

The soundtrack for *Mission Impossible II,* to which Metallica contribute the track 'I Disappear', is released. The band perform 'I Disappear' at the *MTV Movie Awards* three weeks later.

2000
APRIL 13

Metallica file suit against Napster for copyright infringement and racketeering. The case is eventually settled out of court with over 300,000 Napster users banned from the service.

2001
APRIL 23

Metallica, producer Bob Rock and filmmakers Joe Berlinger and Bruce Sinofsky enter the studio to begin work (and visually documenting) the band's next album.

2002
APRIL 14

James, Lars and Kirk appear as guests for the taping of *Aerosmith: MTV Icon.*

2003
FEBRUARY 25

After auditioning many musicians, Metallica announce Rob Trujillo as their new bass player.

2002
JUNE 4

Billed as 'Bob's Band', Metallica take the stage at *Kimo's* in San Francisco with Bob Rock on bass for a short set. The show features several covers, mostly of The Ramones.

2002
MAY 1

Metallica re-enter their newly built studio (christened 'HQ') in San Rafael, California to recommence work on their next album.

2001
DECEMBER 4

James leaves rehab.

2002
MAY 7

Lars and Kirk join Sammy Hagar and ex-Van Halen bassist Michael Anthony on stage at the Fillmore, San Francisco for four songs.

2002
NOVEMBER 12

Live Shit: Binge & Purge is finally released on DVD.

2001
JULY 19

James enters rehab for addiction problems. Recording comes to a swift halt.

2003
APRIL 30

Metallica film the video for their new single, 'St. Anger', at San Quentin prison in front of an audience of inmates.

2003
JULY 4

Metallica begin their US 'Summer Sanatorium' tour in Irving, Texas. Limp Bizkit and Deftones provide support.

2003
MAY 18

Rob makes his concert debut with Metallica when the band plays four shows at San Francisco's Fillmore.

2003
JUNE 6

Metallica's eighth studio album, *St. Anger,* is released. It tops the charts in 30 countries, and produces three singles - the title track, 'Frantic' and 'The Unnamed Feeling' - and an EP, 'Some Kind Of Monster'.

2003
MAY 3

Metallica are selected by MTV to receive their next Icon award.

2003
JUNE 1

Metallica begin a short round of European festival dates, commencing with a headlining appearance at England's Castle Donington.

2003
APRIL 8

Metallica finish work on their new album, titled *St. Anger.*

2004
JANUARY 26

Joe Berlinger and Bruce Sinofsky's documentary *Some Kind Of Monster* debuts at actor Robert Redford's Sundance Film Festival. It goes on to win 'Best Documentary Feature' at the *Independent Spirit Awards*.

2004
JUNE 13

'Some Kind Of Monster' EP is released.

2003
NOVEMBER 3

The 'Madly In Anger At The World' tour commences.

2004
MARCH 15

Metallica are given a Governor's Award from the San Francisco Recording Academy for 'Outstanding Achievement' and 'Creative Excellence'.

2003
DECEMBER 31

Metallica play a New Year's Eve concert in Las Vegas.

2004
JUNE 6

Kirk wins 'Outstanding Guitarist' at the California Music Awards. He celebrates onstage, headlining the 'Download' festival at Castle Donington.

2004
FEBRUARY 8

Metallica win their seventh Grammy award for 'St. Anger', the song taking 'Best Metal Performance'.

2005
FEBRUARY 1

The documentary *Some Kind Of Monster* is released on DVD.

2006
FEBRUARY

Metallica start working through tapes, riffs and song ideas for their forthcoming album with new producer Rick Rubin.

2005
SEPTEMBER 20

Metallica record their voices for an episode of *The Simpsons*.

2005
NOVEMBER 1

Kirk plays alongside Carlos Santana on the track 'Trinity', recorded for the veteran guitarist's latest album *All That I Am*.

2005
JUNE 30

The band launch their own All Metallica Radio Station. The channel plays nothing but Metallica songs.

2006
JANUARY 31

Metallica play a private concert at the Sundance Film Festival at the premiere of *The Darwin Awards*.

2005
NOVEMBER 13-15

Metallica support The Rolling Stones for two dates at San Francisco's SBC Park. These dates are the band's only concert appearances in 2005.

2004
NOVEMBER 28

The 'Madly In Anger With The World' tour concludes in San Jose, California.

2006
SEPTEMBER 10

Metallica appear as cartoon versions of themselves on *The Simpsons*.

2006
SEPTEMBER 29

Kirk's wife, Lani, gives birth to a baby boy named Angel Ray Keala.

2007
APRIL

Metallica enter the studio with Rick Rubin to begin recording their ninth studio album.

2006
NOVEMBER 11

Metallica: The Videos 1989-2004 is released on DVD.

2006
MAY 5

James is honoured with the 'Stevie Ray Vaughan Award' for his support of the MusiCare MAP fund.

2006
SEPTEMBER 30

To mark the 20th anniversary of Cliff Burton's death, a memorial stone created by Manuel Pino is placed at the site where Metallica's tour bus crashed near Ljungby in Denmark.

2006
MARCH 13

Metallica begin their 'Escape From The Studio' tour at New York's Rock 'N' Roll Hall Of Fame. Sixteen dates in all, the stop/start tour concludes in Seoul, South Korea on August 15.

2007
MAY 21

Lars' new partner, Connie Nielsen, gives birth to a baby boy, Bryce Thaddeus.

2008
MAY

Metallica and Rick Rubin conclude recording of the band's new album, *Death Magnetic*.

2007
JULY 8

As part of the tour, Metallica headline London's Wembley Stadium.

2007
OCTOBER 27

Metallica appear at the 21st Annual 'Bridge School' benefit concert alongside Tom Waits, John Mayer and Pearl Jam's Eddie Vedder.

2007
JULY 18

The 'Sick Of The Studio' tour concludes with a sold-out concert at Moscow's Luzhniki Stadium. Metallica return to recording duties.

2007
JUNE 28

Metallica begin their second 'Sick Of The Studio' jaunt at the Super Bock Super Rock Festival in Lisbon, Portugal.

2008
APRIL 15

Metallica's first two albums, *Kill 'Em All* and *Ride The Lightning*, are re-released on vinyl. A re-release of *Master Of Puppets* soon follows.

2008
SEPTEMBER 12

Metallica's ninth studio album, *Death Magnetic*, is released. It immediately goes to number one in 28 countries, selling over 490,000 copies within the first three days in the US alone. Six singles/downloads are later issued, including 'All Nightmare Long' and 'My Apocalypse'.
On the same day *Death Magnetic* is released, Metallica unofficially begin their 'World Magnetic' tour at Berlin's O2 World Arena.

2008
JANUARY 12

After a short Christmas/New Year break, Metallica return to the road in the US for the second leg of their *Death Magnetic* tour, re-opening proceedings at Milwaukee's Bradley Center.

2008
OCTOBER 17

Part one of the US leg of the 'World Magnetic' tour begins at the Cow Palace, Daly City. It will conclude 26 dates later at the Oracle Arena in Oakland, California on 20 December.

2009
MARCH 8

Metallica cancel a performance at Stockholm's Ericsson Globe due to James falling ill. The show is re-scheduled for 4 May.

2008
OCTOBER 28

...And Justice For All is re-released on vinyl. Within a month, *The Black Album* follows suit.

2009
MARCH 29

The video game *Metallica: Guitar Hero* is released.

2008
SEPTEMBER 1

The video for 'The Day That Never Comes', Metallica's first single in five years, is premiered. It is directed by Thomas Vinterburg.

2009
FEBRUARY 22

Metallica win Grammys for 'Best Recording Package' and 'Best Metal Performance' at the 51st Grammy Awards.

2009
JUNE 14

The Metallica tour returns to Europe, opening at the Hartwall Arena in Helsinki, Finland and concluding after 24 dates at the Sonisphere Festival in Knebworth, England on August 2.

2010
SEPTEMBER 15

Following their last round of European shows, Metallica begin the Oceanic leg of the 'World Magnetic' tour at the Rod Laver Arena in Melbourne, Australia. The tour is scheduled to end at the same venue on 21 November.

2009
NOVEMBER 23

Français Pour Une Nuît, featuring Metallica's performance at Nimes, France, is released on DVD.

2009
DECEMBER 12

The fourth leg of Metallica's American tour ends at the HP Pavilion in San Jose, California.

2009
JULY 31

A new intro for the track 'My Apocalypse' is made available as a free download on Metallica's official website.

2010
APRIL 13

Metallica return to Europe for the fifth time, with a date at the Telenor Arena in Oslo, Norway.

2010
JANUARY 19

Metallica return to Latin America, performing at Estadio Universidad Nacional Mayor San Marcos in Peru. Further dates will take the band to Chile, Argentina and Brazil.

2009
JUNE 4-6

Metallica play three dates at Foro Sol in Mexico.

INT

Metallica are one the hardest
working live bands on Planet
Earth. Since their formation in
1981, the 'black dogs' of the
metal movement have probably
played more concert halls,
stadiums, aircraft hangers and
cow fields than any other act of
a comparable nature.

RODUCTION

The backbone to this relentless
touring schedule has always
been the success of their
recorded material, Metallica
albums and CDs becoming
increasingly important and
respected by both fans and
critics as the years unfolded.
Of course, not every Metallica
release can rightly be
described as a classic.
Indeed, there have
been several profound
disappointments to contend
with throughout their career.
Yet, the enduring quality of
the band's output, and their
continued commitment to
testing their own musical
perimeters' underpins their
exalted position within the
rock world.

The facts speak for themselves. The group's first album, 1983's corrosive *Kill 'Em All* virtually ushered in the thrash era of metal – a complex new musical form that relied as much on adrenalised, stop/start time signatures as distortion pedals and histrionic vocals to make its point. Equally, *Kill 'Em All* also marked the end of Metallica 'Mark One', when the band's volatile young guitarist, Dave Mustaine, was fired as much for his chemical dependencies as his frequent personality clashes with front man James Hetfield.

An emotionally bruised yet still defiant Mustaine went on to form Megadeth, an act that would eventually carve their own slice of history within the metal movement. However, his penchant for charging, intense song structures still held huge sway over his old band mates – a truth uncomfortably underlined by Metallica's sophomore effort, 1984's *Ride The Lightning*.

As with many great bands, Metallica survived the loss of a founder member, finding a promising new replacement in guitarist Kirk Hammett. And by 1986, drummer Lars Ulrich, Hetfield, Hammett and bassist Cliff Burton were again at full strength, enjoying a worldwide commercial breakthrough with their landmark disc, *Master Of Puppets*. Again, as it would seem with all great bands, their success was rocked by tragedy when Burton was killed in a road accident.

For many, Cliff Burton's tragic and untimely death spelt the end of Metallica. Yet they persisted, recruiting former Flotsam And Jetsam bassist, Jason Newsted, into their ranks – then returning to the studio to record 1988's *...And Justice For All*, an album that included the international hit 'One'. By 1991, Metallica were one of the biggest acts in the world, their self-titled fifth release (otherwise known as 'The Black Album') eventually selling in excess of 15 million copies.

1996 saw a sea change in Metallica. With *Load*, the band largely abandoned its formative roots in favour of brave new frontiers, adding country and blues

influences to their musical canon. They also re-defined their image, shocking their fan base when – horror of horrors – the group cut their hair, donned eye-liner and some tight-fitting pool-shark suits. 1997's follow-up, *ReLoad*, screwed with existing perceptions still further, Metallica adding folk instrumentation such as hurdy-gurdys and fiddles to their sound. But the hits kept coming and the albums kept selling, 125 million of them. Evidently, the band were living up to their original credo: 'No rules but Metallica rules'.

Their covers album, *Garage Inc.* in 1998 and the following year's *S&M* – a collaboration between Metallica and the San Francisco Symphony Orchestra – were further efforts to loose themselves from the restrictions of their past, both discs asking fans to question what heavy metal could and *should* be. In 2003, they were at it again, re-inventing their sound and status with *St. Anger*, a dense, complex record full of emotionally dislocated lyrics and savage riffing, with Jason Newsted now a fond yet distant memory and new bassist Rob Trujillo bringing unheard of 'funk' influences with him to the group. And then, in 2008, came the long-awaited *Death Magnetic*, which they recorded with legendary producer Rick Rubin. It earned them some of the best reviews of their career and one can only wonder where Metallica will next take their audience.

Metallica: The Music And The Mayhem, then, is not a biography, nor it is intended to be. However, links in theme have been made to ensure continuity, and when important events have occurred in the band's life, they are mentioned. Instead, this book's primary purpose is to explore the music that is Metallica, providing a track-by-track analysis of their recorded career to date – from 'Hit The Lights' to 'All Within My Hands' – each song, each solo, each roar and deathly silence scrutinised and examined, rubber-stamped and indexed.

Enjoy...

KILL 'EM ALL

Music For Nations MFN7,
first released July 1983

Were it not for an acute financial problem, the chances are that the first Metallica album would have been recorded in Los Angeles for the knockdown price of $8,000! Trouble was that Metal Blade Records supremo Brian Slagel couldn't afford it.

Metal Blade was the label on which the *Metal Massacre I* compilation album that introduced the name Metallica to the outside world first appeared. But there were simply insufficient funds for the fledgling label to finance such a major (well, comparatively major) operation at the time. Thus, the band headed east from their Los Angeles base to pursue their dreams and hopes.

It was Ron Quintana and Ian Kallen, co-editors of US fanzine *Metal Mania* and friends of drummer Lars Ulrich, who suggested that the band contact John Zazula (known to the world as Johnny Z), a bear-like figure who was trying to support and promote new heavy metal bands on the East Coast of America.

As luck would have it, Johnny Z had already heard about Metallica through their legendary first demo 'No Life 'Til Leather', now a valuable collectors' item. Johnny ran a small specialist record store in New Jersey at the time and knew that here was a special band indeed – or so he kept telling

anyone he could pin down to listen. So, the situation as it stood was that Lars was trying to contact Johnny, whilst the reverse was also happening! Serendipity or what?!

Once contact had been made (Lars called Johnny, if you wanna know), logistics had to be worked out to allow the band to travel to New Jersey, where Johnny was based. Thus, Metallica were wired $1,500 and Ulrich, guitarist/vocalist Dave Mustaine, guitarist James Hetfield and bassist Cliff Burton began a week-long drive across America – the metal equivalent of Mao Tse-Tung's Long March! During the journey Metallica realised they'd have to get rid of the tiresome, unpredictable and downright dangerous Mustaine.

Once they'd arrived, the band agreed to allow Johnny to sell copies of the *No Life...* demo at a knockdown price of $4.99, which helped finance the setting up of a label to record an album for Metallica. But first there was that little matter of firing Mustaine. Thus, after playing with Venom and Vandenberg in New York, the task fell to Hetfield to confront Mustaine and tell him he was out of the band. Problem was, now they'd taken the plunge and ousted one of the leading lights, who would replace him?

Mark Whittaker, their road manager for the band, told them of a young San Franciscan hotshot called Kirk Hammett, who at the time was playing in another fast-rising local SF outfit going by the name of Exodus. Exodus had actually opened up for Metallica on the West Coast a few months earlier and, having been reminded of Hammett's undoubted prowess via Whittaker's tapes, the remaining trio were convinced his style would fit the band.

Metallica made the approach to Hammett by phone, and offered the chance of recording an album and being in on the birth of something quite sensational, the fledgling axe hero readily agreed to join. He took a red-eye shuttle plane overnight from San Francisco and landed in New York on the day Mustaine was departing.

There followed an intense gigging and rehearsing period, during which the new line-up forged a strong bond. It was obvious they were ready and primed for that first album. Johnny Z had by now signed the band to his newly formed CraZed Management company, alongside New York thrashers Anthrax and venerable new wave of British heavy metal veterans Raven, and he managed to scramble together sufficient funds to put Metallica into a recording studio to start work on their début opus.

It was at the suggestion of Manowar bassist Joey DeMaio that Music America studio, in Rochester, upstate New York, was chosen. The actual studio itself was in the basement of a large club, but of particular interest to Lars was the fact that there was access to a large ballroom on the second floor of the building that would provide him with the huge drum sound he was looking for.

In the end, Metallica spent six weeks in that studio under the production guidance of Paul Curcio, who actually owned the studio – it was cheaper to use the in-house man – at a cost of nearly $15,000. The bill nearly bankrupted a rather panicking Z, who could see the cost simply spiralling away beyond his original budget. And, having failed to find a major label sufficiently interested in what the band was doing to sign 'em up, Z was left out on his own, with the band sleeping on the floor of his tiny New Jersey apartment and the album still in a box of tape in the corner. He was left with no option but to finance the whole recording process from his own far-from-bottomless pockets.

"Maybe I could have gone to someone like Metal Blade or Shrapnel on the West Coast, but this stuff was so new-sounding I didn't know if anyone else would get it, you know?" Johnny once told co-author Mick Wall. "I was like the guy who didn't know if

he had a great idea or a stupid one, and I knew there was only one way to find out."

Thus was born Megaforce Records, started up by Johnny Z as his response to the problem of what to do about his unreleased Metallica tapes. In the States, Megaforce found an ally in Relativity, who agreed to distribute the Metallica album, while over in the UK the newly founded Music For Nations operation similarly contracted to put out the album. But there was still another problem to overcome before that first album would see the light of day. Metallica had wanted to title the opus *Metal Up Your Ass*, with cover artwork depicting an arm coming up through a toilet bowl brandishing a machete – aaarrrggghhh! But Relativity objected, feeling that this would inevitably lead to trouble.

Thus, the band went back to the drawing board. Their response? *Kill 'Em All*, not only their two-fingered 'salute' to those who refused to accept the validity of that initial cover concept, but also the final title, with a suitably bloody cover.

The press reception was rather mixed. Co-author Malcolm Dome, however, saw the potential of the album. Writing in *Kerrang!* at the time, he said: "Mirror, mirror on the wall, who's the fastest of 'em all? Motörhead? Venom... METALLICAaaaaarrrggghh! 'Kill 'Em All' sets a new standard in burn-up freneticism... Metallica know only two speeds: fast and total blur. Yet the remarkable thing about all this is that the band do not use hi-speed tactics to mask either a lack of power or else a dearth of musical technique... Metallica are the craziest bunch of bulldozin', bludgeonin' woaargghh-mongers the American metal academy has vomited up since the days of vintage Ted Nugent..."

Kill 'Em All had seen Metallica make significant strides in changing the face of metal as it had been known. Things, quite literally, would never be the same again!

HIT THE LIGHTS

What a way to introduce Metallica to the waiting world. More than a decade on, this track might sound a little primitive, but there is no doubting the sheer bravura and accurate pacing of the song. 'Hit The Lights' had been one of the stand-out cuts on the *No Life 'Til Leather* demo. Now, given a much more professional production, it still retained that brutal energy and fury. Yet, what really hits home is its severe melodic thrust.

The chugging riff, which owes much to Kiss' 'Detroit Rock City', from Hammett and Hetfield is underpinned by a somewhat eccentric bass line from Burton and the hi-hat oriented drum pattern from Ulrich. For some reason, the rhythm section on this track isn't quite as brutal as it should have been, and Hetfield's first foray into the realm of the lead vocal was slightly hesitant as well, not helped by a ridiculous echo effect in places. Moreover, while we're being critical, the song now seems overlong, extended by a Hammett guitar solo that simply doesn't go anywhere.

Yet, despite these flaws, 'Hit The Lights' was like a breath of fresh air back in 1983. It amply displayed Metallica's roots – taking in the influence of Motörhead, Iron Maiden and Diamond Head – yet proved also that the band had their own inimitable style.

THE FOUR HORSEMEN

When this song first appeared in public, it was under the guise of 'Mechanix'. Co-written by Dave Mustaine, on his departure the band re-arranged the song and changed its title. Thus what we get here is significantly different to the version that first appeared on the *No Life 'Til Leather* demo.

Opening with an Ulrich drum fill, the track quickly gathers speed, ambling along a well-constructed Hammett guitar torrent. But again, there are attempts at time changes which, while bold and innovative, do not come off too well simply because the band were too inexperienced to carry them off. Again Hetfield's vocals are strained and slightly too wispy while his attempts to introduce menace by growling fall flat through a lack of confidence or coaching or both.

At times this sounds like two songs rolled into one. There's the embryonic speed metal facade, underneath which Hammett tries desperately to facilitate a more textured approach.

Again, though, such criticisms are outweighed by the sheer weight of shot and the exuberance with which the band pursued their task. 'The Four Horsemen' was quickly to become a staple of the band's live set.

Strangely, we had to wait a couple of years to hear this song the way it should be recorded. Dave Mustaine chose to record the original version under the title of 'Mechanix' on his first album with Megadeth, *Killing Is My Business... And Business Is Good*. Quite frankly, it blew away Metallica's recorded version completely.

MOTORBREATH

Again a popular number from that ever-present *No Life...* demo, 'Motorbreath' amply lived up to its title, a furious assault on the ears that really saw the band catch fire. For the first time on the album, Metallica seem to be going places.

What impresses most about 'Motorbreath' is that the foursome really gel and ignite. There is a sense within which destiny calls on this track – if that doesn't sound too pretentious – which leads to an understanding of why the band were to become as popular as they are. It is quite magnificent. Lars is punchy and uncluttered behind his kit, Cliff's bass lines rumble without recourse to the mumbling and straying that has often blighted his recorded work, Kirk's guitar solo is consistent and stripped down to the bone, whilst James' voice is comfortable. In short it's a roaring success.

There are moments on 'Motorbreath' that make the hairs on the back of your neck stand up and salute the excitement. For here is proof positive that Metallica were indeed in the business of setting standards that everyone else would have to follow in the coming years. Yet, like most of the material that was drawn from the legendary *No Life 'Til Leather* demo, the original, scratchy version was still better than the first commercially available product. Isn't it about time someone issued that demo?!

JUMP IN THE FIRE

Now here was something to get your teeth into. 'Jump In The Fire' was blatantly, obviously commercial, a melodic edifice that at times seemed to have far too much tunefulness for its own good, but it doesn't work at all, simply because it's too polite. The rhythm and riff owe far too much to early Eighties pop-rock and really don't do the band any favours at all.

'Jump...' was so commercial, at least in comparison to the rest of the album, that it was chosen as the band's first single in the UK. Of more interest to Metallica fans was the B-side of the 12", live renditions 'Seek And Destroy' and 'Phantom Lord'. In the finest tradition of metal music, Metallica actually went into the studio to kick out these two numbers during late October 1983. Then Music For Nations dubbed in applause recorded during a concert at the Marquee Club in London from progressive rock cult figures Twelfth Night!

It might have been a con of sorts, but it didn't concern Metallica fans overmuch. Besides, what 'Jump In the Fire' did for the band was prove they had a commercial ear and were not afraid to exploit it if needed. This side of their character would come even more to the fore during the coming years.

So, is 'Jump...' a failure? Not really. It was just a little too smooth for the young band's own good at this stage in their career. What was needed was little more roughing up. Curcio's production on this cut was too overstated. He seemed to swamp the natural gut power and gunpowder sensitivity of the foursome, making the number a tad too redolent of the NWOBHM. Still, Metallica fans rarely complain about it.

ANAESTHESIA – PULLING TEETH

What a way to reach the mid-way point of your first album. Consider. Metallica were supposed to represent the dawn of a new era in metal, one born of the essential elements of punk's energy and metal's musicianship. Traditional values such as extended solos from the individual musicians were consigned to the dumper. Over and out. See ya. No room in the Eighties for indulgence.

So, what's this track? Essentially a bass solo from Cliff that leads into an instrumental. AAARRRGGGHHH!!! Yet it worked. And how. By this time, Burton's live solo had become a crucial part of the Metallica set. He wasn't a run-of-the-mill bass player. No sir. Burton was an eccentric. Highly unusual and rather unique. Not for him a bass line that complemented what was going on around him musically. He followed his own path, made his own decisions – and that usually meant coming up with something that was a little off the beaten path. It was strange, and with anybody else would have been dismissed as something quite ludicrous. But with Burton the unpredictable actually added to the sum of the musical parts.

When Metallica headlined at the Lyceum Ballroom in London just prior to Christmas 1984, co-author Malcolm Dome was given the opportunity to listen through a headset to what Burton was playing onstage. It was surreal and didn't seem to fit the pattern of whatever song was being played by the others. He was performing in a parallel universe, but it was one that made the band sound even more vicious and approachable by turns. Extraordinary.

Thus, a bass solo from Cliff on 'Kill 'Em All' was almost logical. And he made it work, bringing all his style, talent and individuality to bear on a rumbling, roaring performance that leaps out of the speakers. Listening back now to this track, one is amazed at how vital and vibrant he sounds. And even when the rest of the band jump into the musical fire with him, he still dominates, leading from the front. A true general amidst a phalanx of foot troops!

Sadly, the Metallica bass solo had become such a tradition that when Burton died in tragic circumstances during 1986, the band decided to allow his replacement Jason

Newsted to have his own spot. Almost inevitably it lacked all the roughly-hewn mastery of his predecessor. If ever you want to know whether all the fuss about Burton was fully justified, just listen back to this. Quite magnificent.

WHIPLASH

Ah, 'bang that head that doesn't bang'. That legend appeared on the back of the *Kill 'Em All* album and was inspired by this particular song. This was perhaps the ultimate headbanging anthem.

Supposedly inspired by major Metallica Bay Area fan Rich Birch, this was a pure fist-punching, head-clanking virtuoso exercise in speed metal. Indeed, there are those who believe that the genesis of the term 'thrash metal' lies in this very song. It's a rollercoaster ride of mania, mayhem and madness that doesn't cease from the opening Inter City inter-chordal union between Hetfield and Hammett through to the climactic sunburst of energy as the band virtually collapse in a state of frenzied euphoria. This is the stand-out cut on *Kill 'Em All*, a timeless classic of monster proportions.

Hetfield wails and wrings out each and every word as if his life depends on the venom and spittle he can bring to bear on such lines as "Bang your head against the seat/Like you never did before/Make it ring/Make it bleed". There is nothing subtle about this song, which is perhaps why it became such an instant hit (if you'll forgive the pun) with Metallica fans everywhere.

'Whiplash' has a breadth and depth that is surprising. One of the few true speed metal songs the band have ever recorded, it's the reason why the entire thrash genre grew up around Metallica. They were always more than the sum of that term, but they became the flagship purely because of the craziness they brought to bear on this untethered legion of the damned.

'Whiplash' makes you want to go out and bang your head (the one that doesn't bang) against the nearest hard object. No band has ever captured more perfectly the essence of their appeal in one song. And if one was confronted by a Martian anxious to know what this speed/thrash metal thing is all about, then one could do nothing more reasonable than play this track. It is thrash. It is speed. Nothing more need be said. Even today, no Metallica concert would be complete without it. It is part of Metallica folklore, and even if everything else on this album had been a waste of time, just this track alone would make its purchase worthwhile.

PHANTOM LORD

Anything following on from 'Whiplash' would suffer by comparison. But 'Phantom Lord' didn't try to trade double-barrelled bursts with its predecessor. Rather, it went for a slightly more subtle approach and appearance. This wasn't quite the full-on Metallica some would want, but again it proved the band had a range and variety to their work.

'Phantom Lord' was always popular with metal fans, again like 'Whiplash' simply because it dealt with the subject of metal music itself. A song full of the sort of imagery that dominated the genre at the time – ripping leather, comic-strip violence, misogynistic myth – it was also

a powerful reminder of the lengthy shadow Dave Mustaine still cast over the band. Mustaine co-wrote this track (along with 'The Four Horsemen', 'Jump In The Fire' and 'Metal Militia') and his innate sense of timing and melody can still be heard throughout.

It's often been said that Mustaine had a genius for penning songs that could rip a giraffe's head off its neck at 200 paces, whilst conversely caressing a budgie. And this track is a fine example of the art in question. 'Phantom Lord' booms out, yet also 'neath the bellow there is a slightly softer respect for structure and composition. It is an impressive performance from a band clearly getting right into their stride when it was recorded.

Exactly why Metallica chose to go back into the studio and re-record this number for the alleged live B-side of the 'Jump In The Fire' single is none too clear. Maybe they felt they could improve on what they'd done here. Whatever, the supposed live rendering actually wasn't to be anywhere near as good as the presentation on *Kill 'Em All*. Sometimes the factors that make a song work in one environment cannot be repeated. This was the case with 'Phantom Lord'.

Over the years, this number has fallen out of favour with Metallica. It's a rare occasion if they play it live, which is a pity. It's something of an overlooked masterpiece. Certainly, it enlivens the début album and any Metallica fan not aware of its wiles and wares should immediately check it out.

NO REMORSE

Strange to think that, while Motörhead clearly inspired much of what Metallica were doing at this stage, in 1984 when the 'Head issued a compilation album, they elected to call it *No Remorse*. Were they taking some notice of the young kids on the block? Or was this pure coincidence?

Whatever, this was a fine title for any metal track. And the reality didn't let down the fantasy and aspirations. As was described by

the late Mark Putterford and Xavier Russell in their excellent Metallica biography, this sounded like 'two juggernauts colliding in an echo chamber'. There was little room for subtlety or eclectic nuances here. It was hell for leather, heads down and straight down to the finish line – and it worked a treat.

By the time one reaches 'No Remorse' on the album the listener is left in a state of utter breathlessness simply because of the unrelenting attack; despite the evidence of melody lines, mature arrangements and time changes, the overall impression was of a band out of control – and loving every goddamn minute of it!

Now 'No Remorse' provided yet more evidence that Metallica were locking horns with the most brutal of music in the genre – and goring all the opposition so badly that they might never recover. It's strange to recall that, at the time, this was thought to be so extreme that nothing could possibly go any further. Little did we all know that years later, there would be something almost quaint about numbers such as this, but that's most certainly the case.

But at the time, there was something brutal about 'No Remorse' that fair took one's breath away. In the main, it was due to the fact that Hetfield was fully into his snarling vocal stride. Listening to him bellow his way through this number was akin to getting into a cage with a pride of lions on crack. The chances of getting out with limbs intact is slightly remote!

Essentially, of course, this is a song that seems to revel in the gore and glory of war. Yet 'neath the roaring cannons and piling bodies, there is a sense in which Hetfield (as the lyricist) actually uses the metaphor of warmongering to prove the futility of militaristic actions. The lyrics might be fuelled by a keen blood lust, but they are also scented with irony. When Hetfield blazes about "war without end", he does it with a hint of resignation, as if he's desperately trying to point out that there is a certain inevitable uselessness to it all.

Sadly, much of Hetfield's intricately woven verbiage was probably lost at the time on an audience too busy banging their heads to see any hint of subtlety and pained anti-war feeling in the lyrics of the song. There again, maybe it isn't there anyway and is just a figment of the authors' fevered imagination. Whatever, there is no denying the song has a rightful place towards the very forefront of the Metallica song book – and may even have been a precursor (albeit subconsciously) of the formidable 'One' that was to follow a few years later.

SEEK AND DESTROY

Get those fists in the air. Pound the flesh. Wave the metal banner. for here comes one of the ultimate Metalli-anthems. 'Seek And Destroy' is a flailing, verdant hack'n'slash festival encapsulated in one song. Whilst 'Whiplash' may have perfectly summed up the feel and spread of the Metallica attitude at the time (1983), it was closely followed by this particularly nasty, nascent piece of work.

Amusingly, when it was first introduced to the waiting world on the live front, many in the UK believed it to be called 'She Can Destroy'. This was due to a simple error made on the part of a reviewer for Kerrang! who saw the band live in San Francisco, didn't actually know the song in advance and guessed its title from what he believed Hetfield was singing! Oops, sorry, wrong planet!

Anyway, by the time the mistake had been rectified, 'Seek And Destroy' was well on its way to becoming one of Metallica's most crucial early stage climaxes, a song that leant itself to the old ploy of the 'singalong'. To hear audiences across the world screaming out the refrain "Seeeeaaaarrr-ching, Seek And DESTROY!" is to witness Metallica in their pomp.

So, how does the original recording stand up all these years later? Surprisingly well, as it happens. By the time the band went into the studio to lay down the track they were fully comfortable with the number from numerous live run-throughs – and it showed! No song on the record is performed as tightly and furiously as this one is, even if it now sounds strange

to hear 'Seek And Destroy' without the benefit of a crowd participation sequence.

Given the fact that 'Seek And Destroy' had quickly earned its spurs in the Metallica live set, it's often felt that its presence on this record played a major role in getting the band huge attention in the readers' polls conducted by various European magazines at the end of 1983. Indeed, Kill 'Em All was voted the album of the year by Metal Forces in the UK, with the band collecting the top slot as band of the year in the same publication – not bad for a bunch who were virtually unknown just a few months earlier.

And 'Seek And Destroy' was a big factor. One almost feels compelled to stand in front of a mirror and sing along to this number – it's propulsion is that compulsive.

Incredibly, this track is a shade under seven minutes in length, an amazing situation given the fact that most people regarded Metallica songs as short, sharp shocks back then. But that was the beauty of the band – they could write and perform lengthy epistles without making 'em seem tedious or indulgent.

METAL MILITIA

'Thunder and lightning/The gods take revenge'. Yep, the final track on the first Metallica album went out in somewhat of a blaze of glory, as there was seemingly no let-up in the fury, fire and ire of the band.

"On through the mist and madness/We try to get our message to you," sings Hetfield as the song reaches its climax. And yet again we are talking about a number in excess of six minutes duration!

In many ways, perhaps the band should have ended the album with 'Whiplash', if only because the number was, at this stage in the band's burgeoning career, the epitome of their art and craft. But, no, 'twas 'Metal Militia' that had the honour of bringing the whole shebang to its conclusion.

Overall, Metallica were still coming to terms with the rigours and discipline of studio life. They were under intense pressure due to a lack of money to finish off the recording process as quickly and as painlessly as possible. They had to maintain their energy and muscular strength, whilst adapting to the constraints of a sterile studio environment. Not easy for any young band. Especially difficult for a band who relied so heavily on spontaneity and vibe for their fullest effect.

Strangely, 'Metal Militia' (in itself something of a complex song with a degree of time change few young acts would attempt) stands up better than most on the album to such conditions. Whether this was because the band had adapted to the discipline by the time they came to record this, or whether it was simply an easy song to cut in the studio, it cannot be denied that here was an example of the four working in perfect synchronicity.

The track itself is a straightforward call to arms, although once again there is an underlying feeling that the band were using traditional imagery to make a contemporary, almost cynical point about the manner in which governments can use war to manipulate situations for their benefit. Hetfield even puts certain emphases into the lyrics that accentuate this irony. Of course, this was again lost on the populace because the music was the overpowering, overwhelming strength. The lyrics were seen as no more than onomatopoeic, offering nothing but phraseology for maximum vocal impact – the vocals being seen as a musical instrument and nothing more.

There is of course just the possibility that Dave Mustaine's involvement in the writing of this song had more to do with the subtle undercurrents than any member of Metallica at the time of recording. Mustaine has always had a way with words that suggests he is vehemently anti-war, whilst never actually condemning the exercise. He uses the imagery of warfare to show up its lunacy and ultimate irreverence for that which it is supposed to uphold. So could he have engineered Metallica into this direction without the band themselves realising, as on 'Metal Militia'? An interesting possibility, but one that can probably be dismissed out of hand, if only because Hetfield has continued to use the same poetic attack on subsequent albums, ones that Mustaine was certainly not involved with.

RIDE THE LIGHTNING

RIDE THE LIGHTNING

Music For Nations MFN27 – July 1984

Metallica rode themselves very hard during the latter part of 1983 and the early weeks of '84. They played anywhere and everywhere, especially in Europe. They toured supporting the original UK black metal demons, Venom, and were generally thought to have blown the headlining Brits away at most venues. They appeared at the prestigious Aardshok Festival in Holland on February 11 and again stole the whole show from under the noses of the likes of Venom. And the following day, the Euro-trek ended in Belgium – bedlam in Belgium indeed.

During the course of this trek, the band drew on their début album to provide the backbone of the live set – they were, after all, promoting *Kill 'Em All* – but they did take the opportunity to unveil one new song called 'Ride The Lightning', which concerned the rather serious subject of capital punishment in the States in general, and the use of the electric chair in particular. It was a vexed and contentious subject, but musically, most people agreed, it pointed the way to a massive leap into the future for the band.

Having defined a style of rough-house metal music that set new standards on *Kill 'Em All*, Metallica now seemed to be leaving their past behind. On February 20, they began work on the new album at Sweet Silence Studios in Denmark, with Danish producer Flemming Rasmussen at the helm.

Rasmussen began his recording career at the back end of the Seventies, literally helping to build Sweet Silence with his own hands, and it was he who would finesse their wild thrash into the chopping riffs and extended rhythm shifts that defined the early Metallica sound; the same cacophony countless other young bands would plead for him to repeat, like magic, for them on their own less vaunted studio offerings in the years to come.

"I suppose it was Rainbow who were my first international success," the Dane told co-author Dome. "I engineered their 1983 album *Bent Out Of Shape*." It was hearing this very album that brought Metallica hot-foot to Rasmussen's door.

"I think the band were looking to record their second album in a European studio. I guess Lars (who was born and brought up in Denmark) at the time wanted a break from America. They also wanted somewhere with a resident engineer. The upshot was that they came to Sweet Silence. I was told that they'd chosen this location because they liked the sound I'd gotten for Rainbow.

"I must admit that, at the time, I'd never heard of Metallica. But they sent me some tapes and I loved what they were doing. Mind you, everybody else in the studio thought the band were crap and that I was mad to work with them! We all got on very well, though, clicking immediately as people, which helped a lot. And the fact that Lars was Danish, and also had a big say in what went on, was useful as well. It meant that the two of us could solve certain problems before anybody found out about them!"

The original budget for the album was set at $20,000. Money was still tight within the Megaforce organisation, despite Metallica's comparative success. But this quickly started to escalate beyond $30,000 as the band got stuck into the recording process in earnest. This led to inevitable disagreements between the band in the studio – who didn't want to be

bothered with external monetary problems – and Johnny Z on the outside, who was having to constantly find yet more money to keep the band fed and the bills paid.

"The album took about a month-and-a-half to record," recalls Rasmussen. "During which time all the guys lived in the studio. They were also shopping for a major record deal at the time, which meant you had a number of A&R people popping in and out of the studio, which was an irritation. Eventually, it seemed that they were going to sign with Bronze Records, in London (home, in those days, of Motörhead)."

Bronze seemed convinced that they had a deal with the band all tied up and began to tell the rest of the world about it. However, label boss Gerry Bron blew it when he flew to Copenhagen and, after hearing the album tapes, promptly told Metallica that for release in America the record (which was, at the time, nowhere near completed) would have to be remixed in the US by top producer/engineer, Eddie Kramer.

"Gerry Bron came over, heard what we were doing and didn't like at all," says Rasmussen of that period. "He felt it wasn't quite right and demanded that Metallica had to go over to England and re-record everything. Thankfully, the band refused and didn't sign with Bronze."

Ultimately, everything with Bronze fell apart. The label were looking to snaffle up Metallica for both records and management (with Gerry's son Richard in line as their manager), but their apparent inability to understand and appreciate where the band was coming from had hurt and confused the band. So, after much deliberation and prevarication, they elected to stay with Johnny Z's organisation for management and Music For Nations for record releases in Europe. And the search continued apace for a suitable label in the States to pick up their product.

The band actually took a break from recording to play some shows in the UK during March and April of '84, with Bronze at the time still confident of landing them, before finally finishing off the album with Rasmussen. Then, on June 10, they played a show in Belgium (the Heavy Sound Festival) at which the Bronze company turned up in force, even unveiling a huge banner welcoming Metallica to their label. It was to prove a huge embarrassment to them when they were told that MFN actually had the band signed up for the forthcoming album! Ah well...

"I thought *Ride The Lightning* had great potential," admits Rasmussen. "And most of the songs were pretty good. My favourites? They would have to be 'For Whom The Bell Tolls' – which was actually written in the studio – and 'Creeping Death'.

"After working on that album I got lots of offers from similar bands to Metallica, all of whom wanted that same sound. I turned most of them down, because I didn't want to be stereotyped as a producer who can only work in one style of music. Besides, Metallica were simply the best in their field. Why on earth should I choose to work with imitations when I had the original?!"

While the album came out in Europe during July through Music For Nations (it actually hit the national charts in the UK at number 87 – not in itself spectacular but proof that this form of music could sell), there was something of a question mark over who would eventually release it in the US. Megaforce had put it out and *Ride The Lightning* had done quite well, but there was an increasing rift between Johnny Z and the band. They were unhappy with the lack of promotion and when word rapidly got out, the inevitable happened. Metallica and Johnny Z parted company on rather less than amicable terms. The band signed a management agreement with the mighty Q. Prime organisation in New York (home then of radio-friendly Brit-rockers Def Leppard and US funkmeisters Cameo) and set about sorting out a fully fledged US recording contract for themselves.

Elektra won that particular battle, shaking off heavy opposition to land their quarry. Much of this was due to A&R man Michael Elago, who was a major fan of the band's type of music and clearly understood what it would take to break them in America. Whilst Bronze would have insisted on a complete remix and maybe even re-recording for America, Elago and Elektra saw the album for what it was – a break-through record that might just change the face of metal forever.

Thus, Elektra repackaged and re-issued the *Ride The Lightning* album in the States, and sat back at their executive desks ready to watch it chart.

It's amusing to recall that years later, what is generally regarded as a major watershed album in the history of heavy metal was criticised in certain quarters for being, ulp, wimpy! But that was the case. There were die-hard Metallica fans who just couldn't face up to the fact that their heroes were moving on and developing all the time. But eventually, even the harshest critic had to admit that Metallica had come up with a monster release. Next stop: world domination.

 ## FIGHT FIRE WITH FIRE

Now here's the way to open up your second album – full-on, hell for leather, gung ho action. Led Zep did it with 'Whole Lotta Love' and Metallica didn't hang around as they fired the first salvo on their second opus. 'Fight Fire...' was very much in the style of the *Kill 'Em All* album, a furious, spleen-splitting assault from all angles.

The difference between this song and any number of similarly armoured tracks from that début was, firstly, the production and, secondly, the confidence that came from experience.

Rasmussen was fortunate in that he had an almost state-of-the-art studio at his disposal that was tailor-made for a band like Metallica. They needed a hard, driving, harsh sound that, conversely, allowed some room – not much but enough – for musical sensitivity. Up at Music America Studios on that début, there was a feeling that the sound allowed for a suitably primitive approach but did few favours to the little nuances and pro-active interchanges that were part and parcel of the band. It was fine for the period, but would certainly not have done for Metallica now that they had developed into much more than a young, aspiring act. They were leaders of the new era – and needed the tools to graduate with.

'Fight Fire With Fire' showcased Hetfield's vocals in a manner not previously achieved. His style was now vicious, and virtually took your head off. This was no novice messing around at the gate, but a master literally barging down the gate and storming into town.

As *Metallica – The Visual Documentary* co-author Xavier Russell pointed out about Hetfield when he reviewed the album for *Kerrang!*: "Our heavy Smirnoff (vodka) drinker can still do a fine Arthur Mullard impersonation when he wants to; just check out 'Fight Fire With Fire', although after hearing Hetfield belt out his lines I would have to rename the tune 'Fight Vodka, With Bourbon'!"

The song was inspired (if that is the right word) by the prospect of nuclear devastation, and the track itself allowed sufficient space for Hammett to develop his guitar part, whilst proving tight enough to slam the door in the face of any would-be claimants to Metallica's throne as the undisputed emperors of thrash.

RIDE THE LIGHTNING

The title track had actually been in the can for a while. They first unveiled it onstage long before the album was released and, in fact, it was one of two tracks on the album co-written with the departed Dave Mustaine.

Now, Mustaine had a real feel for melody – as witnessed on all the material he had penned with Metallica – and while it was obvious that the rest of the band had developed away from his original concepts on tracks such as these, nonetheless his unique vision and perception prevails here.

'Ride The Lightning' ostensibly deals with capital punishment, in particular the electric chair. But rather than just using this as a template for a violent assault, the band actually took on the lyrical role of the condemned man, looking at the impending doom through his eyes. This gave the whole song a sense of claustrophobia that was almost suffocating. One can easily lose oneself in this song, such is its momentum, belief and power.

Coupled with this lyrical insight was the music, which never goes too far over the top, but is comparatively laid back, adding to the creeping, sinister foreboding. Hammett allows his guitar part to slither and slide through the

song, displaying for the first time on record an appropriate restraint that set him apart from many of his contemporaries.

Perhaps at this juncture it's worth mentioning that rumours began to percolate through that Hetfield was doing much of the studio lead guitar work, and not the credited Hammett. According to Rasmussen, this was not the case. "James Hetfield is one of the best rhythm guitarists in the world. He could do all the rhythm parts on this, or any other, Metallica album in half the time it would have taken Kirk. But Kirk does all the lead work."

Thus the praise heaped on Hammett's slender yet sturdy shoulders is more than worthy. And with this song, he showed a clean pair of heels to all others in the genre.

FOR WHOM THE BELL TOLLS

For the first time, the band entered the literary world, penning a song inspired by the book of the same name written by legendary macho American novelist Ernest Hemingway.

Now, Hemingway had a great deal to offer any rock band with this novel of sacrifice and abiding if ultimately doomed passion amid the political upheaval of the Spanish Civil War. But for a metal band (let alone a thrash outfit) to take their cue from such a story was a surprise indeed. But that was the beauty of Metallica: they knew no restrictions. They were not prepared just to write about Satan, sex and violence, but wanted to explore other areas of endeavour.

This is what has always made Metallica a band apart from their contemporaries: a need to be adventurous, to look beyond the norm. And they certainly did a magnificent job with this song, turning this epic novel into a worthy number that captured the essence of the story without losing any of the bravura and power by this time associated with the name Metallica.

What's more, this was the first song to really open up their interest in another

20th-century icon, veteran film music composer Ennio Morricone. This Italian genius had made his name by scoring all the great Sergio Leone/Clint Eastwood "Man With No Name" spaghetti westerns, such as *A Fistful Of Dollars*, *For A Few Dollars More* and *The Good, The Bad & The Ugly*. And Metallica had already picked up on his work by using the theme from *For A Few Dollars More* as their intro music prior to taking to the stage.

With 'For Whom The Bell Tolls' there were elements of Morricone's style beginning to creep into their own music – the time changes, the almost gothic acoustic sweeps. This was to be more heavily developed on later albums, and the band were even to sample one of Morricone's themes. According to Lars, it was James who had a particular fascination with the Italian master and pushed the band in this direction. Whatever, it made a pleasant change from just taking influences from the likes of Iron Maiden, Motörhead and Diamond Head, however worthy these bands might have been.

FADE TO BLACK

The title comes from a phrase common to the film world to denote the end of a scene, when the screen dissolves into a black matte. This was an appropriate title for a lengthy, epic tome of the type Metallica have always pursued with a zest, zeal, avarice and style no other metal band could hope to match.

What has always impressed about Metallica is that they are prepared to indulge themselves in lengthy songs that go against the grain. At this point in the mid-Eighties, most bands regarded any song which lasted for more than three minutes as over-indulgent nonsense. There was a tendency to stifle a song at birth if it tried to breathe and open up horizons. Metallica never had such restrictions imposed, either within or without.

That the band actually wrote this in the studio is remarkable in itself. But then maybe that's the point of the song. Had it been written and developed prior to the band entering

TRAPPED UNDER ICE

Originally titled 'When Hell Freezes Over', this number opened up the second side of the vinyl version of *Ride...* in furious style. Whilst there was clearly room for the band to develop new ideas and explore other regions of the musical sphere thanks to numbers like 'Fade To Black', nonetheless what the fans truly wanted to hear from the band at this stage in their career was the blistering, out-and-out thrash stuff. And they certainly got their wish in abundance with this little blazer.

With Ulrich setting the pace behind the kit as if he was being chased down the road by a pack of howling dragons – or debt collectors – the band just let rip. Given their propensity at the time for fuelling up on vodka and other assorted alcoholic beverages, it's entirely possible that this number was actually recorded whilst they were going for broke under the influence. If so, it worked a treat, even if there is an argument for suggesting that maybe it needed a little trimming here and there, just to put into perfect perspective.

The problem with Metallica when they really went for it, as here, wasn't so much the pace of the song in general, but that Hammet could sound as if he was struggling to keep up. And that certainly happens in places. There were times during this era of the band when they were too quick for their own good. But that's what the fans expected – and that's what they certainly got here.

Maybe Rasmussen should have reined them in a little more on a song such as this, but what the hell, how can you really argue with something as truly and gloriously thrashy as this number?

ESCAPE

Following on from the pacey and rather typically metal brutality of 'Trapped...' came 'Escape', which actually had a certain AOR feel to it – amazing though that might seem. Now, there was certainly a degree of internal pressure from the band

the studio, the chances are it would have been cut down in length, simply because they would have had more time to think and reflect. But the incredible pressure of composing in the studio meant that the song was probably allowed to meander beyond the norm, because nobody had the time to sit back and ponder. All of which was to the good of the song.

'Fade To Black' allowed Hetfield to actually sing for the first time on a Metallica song. And it was impressive to hear. Hetfield actually has a rich, resonant voice that at this stage in Metallica's young career had hardly been exposed; he had spent so much time bellowing and growling that one could easily forget that underneath this violent, savage throat lay the seeds of a fine singer.

Aside from Hetfield what made this particular track so outstanding was its brooding, eerie atmosphere, something that built slowly and surely without ever seeming to be stretched beyond reasonable limits. To this day, it remains the basis on which much of Metallica's future success would be based.

to try and break free from the limited media options that were on offer to a band of this ilk. After all, radio airplay was alien to even the most successful of metal acts at the time, so what chance did a 'scumbag' down an' dirty outfit like this one stand? Er, not much.

So, in response, came 'Escape', which over the years has become a forgotten song as far as Metallica fans are concerned. Strange to think that here was a song that had most of us believing it would break Metallica into the bigger arena – and now it's consigned to the dumper.

What impressed about 'Escape' was that it provided a catchy riff on which Metallica could build an almost stereotypical song. It had a clear, defined, obvious structure and could have been covered by Journey or Foreigner. Maybe that was the problem. It was too blatant an attempt at commercialism and didn't impress Metallica fans too much in the long run.

So, just who was the driving force behind this song? Well, it would seem to have been Lars, sensing that here was a golden opportunity to take a great stride towards being more than a quick fix. This was Lars' business head coming to the fore.

At the time of the 'Ride The Lightning' recording sessions, there were strong rumours that the band were, in fact, seriously considering dumping Lars in preference for hotshot Slayer drummer Dave Lombardo. There were those within the Metallica organisation who had serious doubts about Lars' musical abilities. Well, that switch never happened. In fact, years later Lombardo denied that he'd ever been approached.

Ulrich's value to the band was seen on a track like 'Escape'. He had an innate sense of just how they should progress, what they should try and what they shouldn't. Lars might not have been the finest drummer of all time, but he gave Metallica not only a shrewd business head, but also a sense of adventure that

might not otherwise have been so clearly defined. It was he, along with fellow Dane Rasmussen, who encouraged the others to go out on a limb. And while it didn't always work, as indeed on 'Escape', it was a vital part of their developing process.

CREEPING DEATH

The *Ride The Lightning* answer to 'Whiplash'. Well, not totally, but as good as dammit. This was a clenched morning star right through the gut, pure thrash – indeed, arguably the ultimate expression of that genre – and perhaps the last time the band would be so blatantly steeped in the curds and whey of the movement.

'Creeping Death' just roared and rallied the troops with a bursting chorus that defied anybody to ignore it. This was just manic nirvana. Yet, despite the traps inherent in

such an approach, Metallica managed to sound fresh, with Hetfield snarling for all he was worth (a lot) and Burton threatening sound systems across the globe with his monster rumbling bass. And Hammett was in fine fettle on the lead guitar.

'Creeping Death' was to be released as the first single from the album during November 1984, with two very interesting choices of song for the B-side: 'Am I Evil' and 'Blitzkrieg'. These were cover versions of numbers originally recorded by new wave of British heavy metal bands Diamond Head and Blitzkrieg respectively. In the coming years Metallica were to virtually corner the market as far as covers went. But at this stage, it was something new for them – and indeed for anyone else.

Diamond Head had long been a major favourite with Ulrich. Indeed, before he'd even helped to form Metallica he'd followed the Head around on tour in the UK, almost taking in every show they'd ever done. Now it was time to show some form of homage to the Stourbridge band, who sadly made little commercial impact themselves.

The choice of 'Am I Evil' was fairly obvious really. Not only was it the most popular of all Diamond Head's material, but it was also their heaviest number, one that leant itself admirably to Metallica's inimitable treatment. And, sure enough, the Californians did DH proud on this one. In fact, the heaviest irony about this cover version was that it became so much a part of Metallica folklore that most people actually believed it was their own song. Indeed, to this day most Metallica fans would be hard pushed to name who did the original.

This is one case where the cover version eclipsed the original – and that doesn't happen very often. Metallica were to go on to do another two Diamond Head songs, 'Helpless' on the seminal EP *The $5.98 EP: Garage Days Re-revisited* in 1987 and 'The

Prince' for the B-side of 'Harvester Of Sorrow' a year later, but this still remains their fiercest and finest cover.

Blitzkrieg were a rather more obscure NWOBHM act, again personal favourites of Lars', whose choice of covers dominated at this juncture in their career. Blitzkrieg themselves hailed from Leicester and sadly made very little lasting impact on the metal scene. Unlike Diamond Head, they gained nothing from the patronage of Metallica, except the royalties due for this cover. In truth, again unlike Diamond Head, Blitzkrieg didn't really have that much to offer the world, except for their eponymous anthem. And again, this now firmly belongs to Metallica.

It's probably fair to say that Metallica began a whole trend towards cover versions on the B-sides of singles and beyond with these two numbers. They were far from the first to do this (Iron Maiden had done it previously, and this might have inspired Metallica to take the plunge), but the impact they made, especially via 'Am I Evil' (which remains to this day a highlight of their live set) has led to cover versions becoming the norm in metal circles.

THE CALL OF KTULU

What a way to finish off an album. An instrumental based on an obscure series of stories by American fantasist HP Lovecraft. And it worked, leaving the listener breathless for more.

The song was effectively the valedictory contribution from Dave Mustaine, and it's a monumental piece of work, almost orchestral in style and content. Just why there were no lyrics to this slow-burning masterpiece remains open to rumour and hearsay. It has even been suggested that Hetfield did start to pen lyrics, but didn't quite know what to write because he'd never actually read any of Lovecraft's stories! Whether this is true or myth is open to debate – it is very unlikely that, should the band have wanted lyrics to fit this number, they would be incapable of coming up with any.

'The Call...' actually has the feel of a jam session tightened up in the studio. Indeed, again it has been suggested that this was only dragged out because the band needed something to finish off the record and were running out of time and money. Thus, in desperation they pulled out a half-finished tune from the Mustaine era and did their best to bring it up to speed. Again that remains unconfirmed.

Whatever, the song works in this form. You do not need lyrics to make it work. However, should you require them then you can do no better than to delve into the original Lovecraft stories on the Cthulhu mythos (note the difference in spelling). So, just who was this character HP Lovecraft? Well, his full name was Howard Phillips Lovecraft, who was born and lived in New England. He wrote his stories during the first part of the 20th century, and the Cthulhu cycle of stories was based on an ancient mythology he created himself from scratch. They have become classics of the fantasy genre, and the perfect fodder for bands such as Metallica.

'The Call Of Ktulu', whilst a little different in construction and approach for Metallica, proved to be the best way to finish off what has become one of the cornerstones of the thrash genre. Metallica went on to make bigger and better albums, but perhaps none that was to have the same impact on a whole generation of budding musicians.

MASTER OF PUPPETS

Music For Nations mfn60 –
Released March 1986

Master Of Puppets marked the end of an era for Metallica; the end of a band that didn't take itself too seriously, and the beginning of another that took itself very seriously indeed. It was an attitude that reflected their new-found status as the agenda-setters of thrash.

Nevertheless, they were determined not to lose sight of their objectives. Metallica's success, Lars was always the first to acknowledge, was as much to do with timing, as it was the noise they were making. "There weren't really any independent labels in America when we were starting out in the early Eighties. And everything would have to go through the major record companies, who would package you in a way they thought was saleable to the public," he recalled.

"But we said 'Fuck that' and just plodded on doing our own stuff and feeling great about it. Early on we had a very distant attitude to the business side of things. We always stood our ground about what we played, how we looked, how we presented ourselves. Or how we didn't present ourselves.

"All the people got to hear about back then was shit like Styx, or REO Speedwagon or whatever... and then we came out and I guess people thought, 'Wow, where has all this shit come from? How come we haven't heard this before?' Because the major record companies never believed that anything like that could actually sell, that's why!"

Certainly neither Lars Ulrich nor Metallica have ever pretended that anything less than total world domination by lunch-time was their intention. But with the arrival of the third Metallica album, previously thought unattainable goals were suddenly being reached. *Master Of Puppets* wasn't just the first Metallica album to creep like death into the Top 30 of the US charts (it made No. 41 in the UK), it was the first Metallica album that anybody other than battle-hardened thrash-heads had felt drawn to investigate with any degree of seriousness.

Released in the same year as Bon Jovi's enormously successful *Slippery When Wet* album – corporate Reaganomic rock at its apotheosis, surely – *Master...* still stuck out like a badly bandaged thumb. But this time there was more to it than a kitsch B-movie appreciation of the fact that the band was deliberately going against the grain. The quality of the material ensured them at least of that.

Listening to the title track for the first time, or something as wilfully sinister as 'Disposable Heroes', it was plain that the bunch of noisy kids with too many beers in them had vanished to be replaced by a rock band of startling rhythmic power and remarkable (if somewhat inverted) melodic grace.

Recorded once again at Flemming Rasmussen's beloved Sweet Silence studios in Copenhagen, with the producer once more at the controls, the eight tracks on *Master Of Puppets* found Metallica at their most accomplished and confident yet. Stretched over 50 minutes (which in those pre-CD days was almost unheard of, most vinyl albums coming in at around the 40-minute mark), this was early, Cliff-era Metallica both at their most indulgent and their most creative. Never again would they sound this downright dangerous.

"If you look back on the albums, next to the song titles the times are always listed," recalled Lars with a rueful smile. "I used to be really proud of it. In the past, we'd do a rough version of a song and I'd go home and time it and go, 'It's only seven and a half minutes!' I'd think, 'Fuck, we've got to put another couple of riffs in there.' Now I'm not bothered either way."

Mixed by Michael Wagener in Los Angeles, *Master...* was, conversely, both state-of-the-art thrash metal and Metallica's first tentative step towards transcending the genre they had themselves had a huge hand in creating.

"I don't think the word 'thrash' ever really applied to us anyway," Lars announced somewhat contrarily at the time, handily ignoring the fact that just two years earlier he had boasted that *Kill 'Em All* was probably one of the most influential thrash metal albums of all time.

"Sure, we were the originators of the style because of the speed, energy and obnoxiousness in our songs. But we always looked beyond such limitations and were better defined, I think, as an American outfit with European attitudes to metal. Quite honestly, I'm rather fed up with the mentalities shown by so many thrash acts; all they wanna do is play faster and faster. What does that prove? Anyone can concentrate on speed for its own sake, but this doesn't allow any room for subtlety, dexterity or growth. Metallica are always seeking to improve, which is why we are getting attention now."

First released worldwide on March 7, 1986, the band celebrated its release by landing the support slot on a five-month tour of America opening for Ozzy Osbourne, the most prestigious support spot on offer that summer.

"That was a real break for us," Lars admitted later. "At the time, Ozzy was perceived as one of the most controversial metal stars in the US – he drew a really extreme type of crowd... which suited us down to the ground, because here we were as this even more extreme up-and-coming metal band that Ozzy was giving his kind of seal of approval to by taking out on tour with him."

The arrangement worked well for both artists and by August of 1986, *Master Of Puppets* had officially gone Gold in America in recognition of over 500,000 copies of the album sold. Still, there were no videos to promote the album, and little if any mainstream radio play to keep them in the public eye after the show had left town.

"We've been asked to do a video but the whole idea just makes us cringe," Lars would always wince when the subject came up. In many ways the Eighties equivalent of refusing to release a single (as many heavy rock artists of the Seventies had done), Metallica's refusal to make a video to help promote their first three albums simply added to their growing enigma.

As Lars would admit years later: "We got more publicity from not doing a video than doing a video. We just said, 'Well, the formula for record company stuff is here's the band, here's the look, here's the safe radio song and here's the video.' We just thought, 'Fuck that'. It took us a long time to realise that you can use a video as more than just the obligatory promotion tool. You can use the medium and make it as much fun and creative as it is to make a record. So on the next album we sat down and made a video that was as creative and fun as when we make a record. And not just have some kind of... running down a corridor with the wind in your hair bullshit.

"But at the time of *Master Of Puppets*, we just couldn't see the point. We'd rather spend the money we would have spent on a video keeping the band on the road and working that way."

Value for money was always a major consideration where Metallica was concerned. Lars had always been impressed when his own favourite bands had taken trouble over an album sleeve or a stage show, and he was determined to put Metallica in the same fan-friendly niche.

When the band began headlining their own shows in Britain right after the Ozzy tour, they would often turn in a two-hour-plus set, extending already often over-extended album versions into live epics of distortion and pounding, machine-gun rhythms. Once asked by co-author Wall whether Metallica would ever consider shortening their live concerts a tad, James Hetfield scowled as he considered the question, as if for the first time in his life.

"Some, maybe. If we're boring people, sure." He flashed the sort of look you might expect to find on a 'Wanted' poster. "It's not the time we think about, it's the songs we play on the night," he explained curtly. "Some fuckers come up after shows and say shit like, 'Hey, man, how come you didn't play 'Disposable Heroes'?' You think, 'Goddamn, you wanna sandwich, too?!' We always play for two or three hours,

man, and there's still some people who aren't happy with it."

Metallica's 1986 UK tour had begun with a long show at St. David's Hall, Cardiff, on September 10, with New York thrashers Anthrax in support (Metal Church's John Marshall deputised for James on rhythm guitar while the guitarist nursed his still-plastered wrist, broken in a backstage skateboarding accident towards the end of the Ozzy dates). The fans raved; the critics ranted. And suddenly yesterday's joke band was tomorrow's promised land.

A major turning-point for the band on every level, *Master Of Puppets* was also, tragically, the last Metallica album to feature the playing and influence of Cliff Burton.

The band's last date of the UK tour had been at London's Hammersmith Odeon, on September 21. Two days later they took off for Scandinavia and the start of what was to have been a month-long European tour. Travelling on their tour bus through the night of September 27, having just completed a show at the Sonahallen in Stockholm, the third date of the tour en route to the next show at the Saga, in Lars' hometown of Copenhagen, the bus skidded off the road near the small Danish town of Ljungby and toppled onto its side into a ditch. Cliff, who was sleeping in one of the bus's eight bunks, was thrown through the side-window as the bus toppled onto its side and was crushed to death. He was just 24.

According to the official Danish police report, the driver was arrested as a matter of course, as Danish law requires, but later released without charge after their investigations revealed that the real cause of the crash was black ice on a particularly nasty bend in the road.

At first, Metallica considered packing it in, unable to reconcile themselves to the loss of their friend. In many ways, Cliff was the

Galloping drums, toothache guitars and slit-eyed vocals delivered straight from the lip of the toilet-seat, 'Battery' is a frankly unpretty song about the light that burns within despite the violent darkness without. A half-breed, 'Battery' is a nasty collision between punk and metal that made few concessions to either rigidly defined culture. It only really made sense when you were down the front, you and the stormy sea of crushed humanity bobbing and weaving dangerously around you. That's when you knew exactly what James meant as he spat out the words: "Smashing through the boundaries/Lunacy has found me/Cannot stop the battery..."

Some of us still have the scars to prove it ...

 ### MASTER OF PUPPETS

Alongside 'Creeping Death', 'Enter Sandman', 'One' and 'Fade To Black', this is one track that Metallica will doubtless feel duty-bound to play live for the rest of their days. Quite simply, it's a classic; one of the greatest heavy metal numbers of all time.

Built around one switch-blade simple riff, 'Master Of Puppets' captures the Cliff Burton-era Metallica sound at its pinnacle of over-the-top perfection. It could quite easily have ended on a brutal fade-out after three minutes 35 seconds, and it would have been a classic to lie proudly next to earlier generation killer-dillers like Black Sabbath's 'War Pigs', or Deep Purple's 'Fireball'.

Instead, in finest Cliff-era Metalli-style, things are only beginning, and the riff is momentarily extinguished while Kirk and James descend into out-and-out melodrama as they proceed to squall their guitars in unison for another three-and-a-half minutes like a pair of heartbroken alley cats bemoaning their fate.

Then, just as you decide you've had enough and they're either going to stop or you're going to kill yourself, slowly but surely the band pounds its way out of the muddy emotional rut and drags the song back

tough guy of the band, the one who was never intimidated by the size of the crowd or the staid conventions of the corporate mid-Eighties record business. He was, quite literally, irreplaceable. And though they would inevitably decide to bring in a new bass player and see through what they had begun, things would never be the same again.

 ### BATTERY

For such a cataclysmic release, *Master Of Puppets* began in a surprisingly subdued manner, managing to capture that strange quiet before the storm that ends the world with an acoustic bit of nonsense that recalled their kitsch obsession with the heroic wild west motifs of Ennio Morricone's more melodramatic moments.

It wasn't to last. Kirk Hammett's lead guitar breezes in like a foul wind as the song begins to shed its reflective acoustic posture for an all-out electric assault that really does work like a battering ram to the head.

1963

December 26
Lars Ulrich born in
Gentofte. Demark.

1962

February 10
Cliff Burton born in Castro Valley, California.

1962

November 18
Kirk Hammett born in
San Francisco, California.

1963

March 4
Jason Newsted born in
Battle Creek, Michigan.

1963

August 3
James Hetfield born in Downey, California.

1973

February
Lars sees Deep Purple with his
father Torben in Copenhagen. It
is his first rock concert.

1981

May 9
James and Lars meet for the first time at
Newport Beach, California.

1978

James joins his first band, Obsession,
with Jim Arnold, Rich and Ron Veloz.

1982

January
First original Metallica song,
'Hit The Lights', is recorded.

1981

October 15
Lars and James form Metallica.
Lead guitarist Dave Mustaine soon
joins them after responding to an
advertisement in *The Recycler*
newspaper. They make Los Angeles
their temporary home.

1982

March 14
Metallica play their first
concert at Radio City,
Anaheim, California with new
bassist, Ron McGovney.

1983

April 1
After continuing personality clashes with Dave Mustaine, Lars, James and Cliff ask Kirk to join Metallica. Mustaine plays his last gig with the band nine days later.

1982

December 28
Having seen bassist Cliff Burton onstage with his latest band, Trauma, at Los Angeles club Whisky A Go Go, Hetfield and Ulrich ask him to join Metallica. After some consideration, Cliff agrees.

1983

July 16
Kill 'Em All is released. The record will sell over three million units in the next decade. Two singles from Kill 'Em All, 'Whiplash' and 'Jump In The Fire', are also released.

Go'morron!

Ny buss lyft för markarydsföretag SIDAN TOLV

Olja bättre än gas hävdar Pilkingtons MITTEN

SMÅLÄNNINGEN

3:50

Nr 187   Vecka 40   Måndagen den 29 september 1986

Två svåra olyckor på lördagen

ROCK-stjärna dödades

Cliff Burton, basist i uppmärksammade hårdrockgruppen Metallica dödades när turnébussen for av vägen och slog runt.

Den amerikanska hårdrockgruppens Europaturné slutade i djup tragik vid en dödsolycka på E 4 vid Dörarp på lördagsmorgonen.
Cliff Burton, 24-årig basist i gruppen Metallica, krossades till döds under turnébussen, när den körde av vägen. Chauffören anhölls på lördagsefter-

middagen, misstänkt för vårdslöshet i trafik och vållande till annans död.
Rockgruppen var på väg i en stor engelskregistrerad buss från en spelning i Solna till en konsert i Köpenhamn.   SIDAN SEX

Ljungbybo svårt skadad

1985

September 1
Metallica begin recording their third album, *Master Of Puppets,* again at Copenhagen's Sweet Silence Studios. Fleming Rasmussen produces.

1986

September 27
While en route from Stockholm to Copenhagen, Metallica's tour bus crashes. Cliff Burton is killed in the accident.

1986

September 10
The 'Damage Inc.' tour arrives in Europe with a date in Cardiff, Wales. Eleven days later, Metallica make their first headlining appearance at London's Hammersmith Odeon.

1984

September 12
Metallica sign a new record deal with Elektra Records, who re-release *Ride The Lightning* on November 16.

February 22
Metallica win 'Best Metal Performance' for their
cover of 'Stone Cold Crazy' at the Grammys.
Rob Trujillo's band, Suicidal Tendencies, are also
nominated in the same category.

1991

August 12
Metallica's new self-titled record is released.
It becomes known as *The Black Album*.
Débuting at number one in both the UK and
US charts, it will spawn five hit singles and
sell over 22 million copies worldwide.

1988

August 25
...And Justice For All is released.
Despite its curious production values,
the album reaches number six in the
US charts, going on to sell over eight
million units. When released in the
UK in September, the record peaks at
number four.

2001

July 19
James enters rehab for addiction problems. Recording comes to a swift halt.

2000

April 13
Metallica file suit against Napster for copyright infringement and racketeering. The case is eventually settled out of court with over 300,000 Napster users banned from the service.

1997

January 26
Lars marries his girlfriend, Skylar, at a ceremony in Las Vegas.

1997

August 17
James marries his girlfriend, Francesca.

2009

March 29
The video game *Metallica: Guitar Hero* is released.

2007

May 21
Lars' new partner, Connie Nielsen, gives birth to a baby boy, Bryce Thaddeus.

2008

September 12
Metallica's ninth studio album, *Death Magnetic*, is released. It immediately goes to number one in 28 countries, selling over 490,000 copies within the first three days in the US alone.

2010

September 15
Following their last round of European shows, Metallica begin the Oceanic leg of the 'World Magnetic' tour at the Rod Laver Arena in Melbourne, Australia. The tour is scheduled to end at the same venue on 21 November.

into that neck-snapping riff, the hook going through you like a train.

The lyrics, as ever, were layered with meaning. You could read it as a straight passion play, a plea for sanity in a control-freaked world. You could take it as the latest anti-establishment instalment of a saga that began with 'The Four Horsemen', continued with 'Creeping Death' and now found its doomed catharsis in 'Master Of Puppets'.

Or you could see it simply as one young band's way of expressing its determination not to be led by the nose down anybody's weird path but their own.

"Taste me you will see/More is all you need..." roars James on the chorus and it is impossible, however ironic he is being, not to agree with him.

THE THING THAT SHOULD NOT BE

After the wall-shaking opening brace of numbers, 'The Thing That Should Not Be' offers something of a minor respite from the heavy-duty chaos that surrounds it, the band labouring menacingly over a corkscrew riff that works its way into your consciousness slowly before blooming like a black rose. The topic under discussion here, apparently, is the madness that is said to live at the bottom of the well of all human souls; the untrained animal within; repellent darkness and a too-shallow sea; the thing that should not be. But is.

Listened to on its own, removed from the context it thrives in on the album, 'The Thing ...' is not an overwhelmingly remarkable number, being workmanlike and far from the classic cross-boned riffing of more established Metalli-headbangers.

But returned to the darkly heroic context of the rest of the *Master...* album, it assumes a more fitting grandeur. If life was like the flame of a candle, this would be the hot melted wax it leaves behind...

WELCOME HOME (SANITARIUM)

Another stone cold classic. Beginning with the lonely chime of a treated guitar note, the track begins slowly, snaking up on you through the moon-grass. Once again the world is a lunatic asylum and the subject is madness-as-metaphor for honesty and truth, the patient as imprisoned by his knowledge as the one-eyed man in the kingdom of the blind: both can see a sky no-one else will even acknowledge exists.

Then, just as the mood threatens to quicksand into irretrievable gloom, everything suddenly changes and Lars' drums come storming in like the bewildered cops in the last reel of a zombie movie and the whole thing takes off into a ride through all the dead stars still left twinkling in the cold night sky.

The message was simple but horrible: this was truth, not as liberator but as impaler. Love as hate. Black as white. Life as death. Like a bad dream, it had become a recurring theme in all of James Hetfield's lyrics.

Yet it was the kind of haunting of the senses you could only welcome onto your stereo with a certain sense of gratitude. This was 1986 and nothing else sounded even half this mad.

DISPOSABLE HEROES

More punk metal thrashing featuring James' extraordinary hand-chopping rhythm work. This time the theme is the depressing reality of being a foot-soldier caught up in a war you don't really understand, being required to kill people or be killed by those that you don't really know, in a land you cannot understand and will surely never want to know again.

"Hell is here," James intones solemnly. "I was born for dying!" he wails brokenly. It is a subject that James Hetfield and Metallica would return to more than once over the years, but with the honourable exception of the track that would become the single from their next album ('One'), they would never do it with such eloquent force as they do here.

At nearly eight-and-a-half minutes, 'Disposable Heroes' is hard, heavy and with the whiff of genuine terror hanging over it like a death sentence: a quintessential moment on an album crammed with such half-light classics.

LEPER MESSIAH

Of course, the battlegrounds that Metallica write their songs about are not just those you find on some far-flung, bombed-out horizon. "War starts at home," co-author Wall remembers James Hetfield telling him when they met in Copenhagen during the making of *Master...* When asked to elaborate, James simply hissed: "You watch TV, doncha? Well, there's war right there every night. You have to be on your guard or that shit's gonna get you every time..."

He wasn't being too specific at the time, but listening back to 'Leper Messiah', it seems appropriate to recall that quote here as this track deals specifically with the mortal danger in which viewers undoubtedly place their souls while watching the now largely discredited Born Again Christian TV channels that were just then beginning to dominate the news in America.

"The thing is, we don't just write songs about Satan and demons and all that shit like so many of the bands we're supposed to have inspired," Lars explained at the time. "Or if we do sing about Satan then we sing about the Satan that everybody with eyes can actually see at work right now on this earth.

"What those so-called Christian fundamentalists represent, to us, is a very real evil. Trying to put fear into the population. Fear of being in any way different from the norm – which is probably the healthiest thing in the world to be.

"And what these TV preachers are about is even more bizarre. They don't just wanna fuck you up, they want you to give them all your money for doing it, too! That's what I call truly disgusting. And 'Leper Messiah' is just an attack on that whole weird scene..."

One that more than hits its target.

ORION

A difficult track to review, this one, as it is a bass-led instrumental written mostly by Cliff Burton and features a quite beautiful extended bass guitar passage two-thirds of the way through quite unlike any other bass solo the authors have ever heard. No over-impressed-with-itself thumb-twanking; no obtuse flights of funk-a-tron fancy.

In fact, it hardly sounds like a bass guitar at all, which is probably what Cliff, the consummate bass guitarist, was aiming for. Fading in, fading out, 'Orion' is a moment of almost glistening wonder, a spectral zone into which thoughts congeal and emotions are allowed to ebb and flow, to exhale the hate.

'Orion' is the small white spot in the ocean of black the band veils the rest of the album in, made all the more poignant by the fact of its author's tragic demise just six months after its release.

DAMAGE INC.

"After *Master Of Puppets* came out, I was surrounded by bands all begging me to give them the sound that Metallica got with that album," producer Flemming Rasmussen would recall years later. "But of course it was impossible! To get that sound, you had to have been that band at that moment, because they were inventing it all on the spot."

And though it is tempting, in retrospect, to marvel at the tremendous job Metallica did in meshing the thunder of heavy metal to the gritty realism of punk rock, as Rasmussen implies, nobody was that sure of what they were doing.

Which is why a track like 'Damage Inc.', the ultimate track on the ultimate Cliff Burton-era Metallica album, was such a shock. Where tracks like 'Creeping Death' and 'Fade To Black' from *Ride The Lightning*, or 'Seek And Destroy' and 'Whiplash' from *Kill 'Em All* had been universally admired for their superior blend of strong lyrics and take-no-prisoners

rock music, 'Damage Inc.' was something else again.

Played at an almost psychotic speed, sheet metal riffs making instant craters in your cranium, James snarls the lyrics and dares you to make sense of them. Shoved against a wall, the song seems to be about what happens when someone simply gives up the ghost and decides they don't care enough to live any more, so they might as well take as many down with them when they die.

"Blood will follow blood!" James screams at the top of his lungs at the nasty climax. "Dying time is here..."

It was a brilliant, brutal and sadly prophetic way to end the album that brought the significant, pre-platinum Metallica era to a sudden, jagged end.

It was killer.

...AND JUSTICE FOR ALL

Vertigo VERH61 – September 1988

Following the breakthrough success of *Master Of Puppets*, suddenly, whether they liked it or not, the pressure was on Metallica to come up with a credible follow-up. And not just as a sequel to their best album but as proof positive that, in the wake of Cliff's death, the band itself was still alive. At such a moment, most bands would probably have been pleased to carry on with as few major changes to the background scenery as possible.

Instead, Metallica stoutly refused to stick to the old showbiz maxim of you-don't-fix-what-ain't-broke and more or less changed everything in sight for the making of this, the most important album in their career.

Of course, the most significant change had been forced upon them: the need for a new bassist. Former Flotsam And Jetsam member Jason Newsted had been worked into the band's recording environment via the *Garage Days Re-visited* EP – a five-track collection of cover versions released in the summer of 1987 while the band took part in that year's Pan-European 'Monsters Of Rock' festivals, and their first release under their new major record deal (Elektra in the US; PolyGram for the rest of the world). But this was the first time he had participated in a fully-fledged Metallica album and Jason must have known how the hardcore Cliff-fans would be waiting with their arms folded for him to try and impress them.

Given this almost impossible task, Newsted was further hampered by being, through no apparent fault of his own, the most anonymous presence on *... And Justice For All*. Simply, you can't really hear him. The mix doesn't allow you to. Which is doubly unfortunate as, firstly, Jason is a bloody good bass player, as time would prove, and, secondly, Cliff's bass had established a massive presence in the mature Metallica sound, a warmth and humour that was simply not there any more on the album that followed without him.

And, originally, there was to be a new producer and a new studio to record in as well.

"The band were keen to get Mike Clink in, because they loved what he'd done for Guns N' Roses on the *Appetite For Destruction* album," Flemming Rasmussen recalled without rancour. "But it simply didn't happen for them." Flemming had been asked if he would stand-by as a last-minute replacement should the situation with Clink not work out, and the gentlemanly Rasmussen had agreed. "That was OK. I could understand their feelings."

When things with Clink failed to match up to expectations, Lars was straight on the phone to Copenhagen. "I got a call from Lars, asking me to come over straight away, because there were huge problems," Rasmussen said. He was on a plane to Los Angeles the very next day. "The band had really wanted to get this album done very quickly, but had become bogged down in the studio."

Starting again from scratch, Flemming admits he was concerned over how much things might have changed since Cliff's death. "You see, he was one of the best bassists in his field because he was such a madman. But Jason Newsted has his own strengths, on which I could work."

What had altered, said Rasmussen, was the set up of the band. "Lars and James had

taken over a lot more. They decided what was going on."

Recording began in earnest with Flemming at One On One studios, in Los Angeles, at the beginning of 1988. By April, the band were ready to reveal the title of their next album: ...And Justice For All. The final line from the Declaration of Independence, it is used here as cynical metaphor for the more general theme of injustice that pervades the entire record.

As Lars told co-author Wall: "We're a band of extremes. We move between this really serious album to a stupid cover version EP, back to something more involved like this... otherwise we get bored so easily."

Not to everybody's taste when it was finally released in September 1988, the production seemed to clunk too often when it needed to clank; it crunched when it should have cranked. Mostly, it sounded wooden, tinny, as flat as an autobahn and, in some cases, almost as tedious, though Rasmussen will go to his grave defending it.

"The band wanted a certain style at the time and they got exactly what they asked for. The four of them thought they were making something brilliant. But once the record was finished, they felt that it wasn't really what they were after at all. But I don't think it was as bad as some people have made out. Besides, for the half-a-year after its release every other album in the genre sounded like ...And Justice For All, so it couldn't have been that awful!"

The fourth Metallica album was preceded by the single, 'Harvester Of Sorrow', backed on its various formats by yet more cover versions, this time of Budgie's ancient garage anthem, 'Breadfan', and Diamond Head's forgotten early Eighties romp, 'The Prince' – both tracks that originated from the brief period when Mike Clink had been in charge of the sessions. The single reached number 20 in the UK. But it was the slightly more radio-friendly 'Eye Of The

Beholder' that devoted rock stations like KNAC in Los Angeles immediately picked up on in America.

The band had brought an added air of expectancy to the release of their new album by embarking on that summer's US version of the 'Monsters Of Rock' festival, trekking around some of the biggest outdoor stadia in the US on a bill that also featured Van Halen, The Scorpions and management-mates Dokken, and premiering new tracks from the forthcoming album. When reports came back that Metallica were selling as many T-shirts at the shows as Van Halen, even the most cynical eyebrows in the record business were being raised.

The sold-out world tour of their own that followed, which arrived in Britain in October 1988, featured a ludicrous theatrical replica of the Statue of Liberty (quickly nicknamed 'Edna') decorating the stage – which collapsed melodramatically at the endless climax to ... And Justice For All each night, by which time everybody was quite delighted to see the monstrosity's head fall off.

Nevertheless, the album, released worldwide on September 6, 1988, was a huge commercial success, reaching number four in both Britain and America. Nevertheless, the recording and the 18 months of touring that followed its release had taken its toll.

"When we were in LA doing the Justice album, I just flipped out, couldn't hang with it anymore," James later recalled with a still-dazed shake of the head. "On the 'Damaged Justice' tour I had stress problems, booze problems, my stomach got really fucked up. As soon as I stopped drinking, though, my head started clearing out and I realised what the fuck was going on. These days I'm much better at dealing with shit like that."

When, in February 1989, the band released 'One' with their first promotional video to

accompany it, at the start of their first headline tour of America, it looked like Metallica had their first US hit single on their hands, too. Featuring old black and white footage from the Hollywood version of Dalton Trumbo's eerie epic, *Johnny Got His Gun* inter-cut with stark, strobe-lit shots of the band performing the song in what looks like an underground bomb-shelter, it perfectly captured the torturous emotions the song conveys so convincingly.

For a first video, 'One' was shockingly accomplished. It stunned you the first time you saw it and would continue to do so with equal ferocity every other time you found it before your troubled eyes. Frightening and magnificent, 'One' would eventually garner the band their second Grammy award (they received their first for their blistering cover of Queen's 'Stone Cold Crazy' on the Elektra anniversary compilation album released the same year).

What had made them change their minds and agree to finally record a video, though? Commercial pressure? To a degree, yes. The world (at least as MTV knows it, anyway) was certainly ready for a Metallica

video by 1989. And also, as Lars would later explain to co-author Wall, simply refusing to make a video just for the sake of it was its own "self-made cross".

"First it was because we couldn't afford to. Then it was because we didn't want to – like, we're Metallica, you don't tell us what to do, kind of thing," said Lars. "But everybody should know by now that we get really bored easily with things we do. We're a band of extremes. And we keep changing, keep following our instincts in whatever direction our heads take us. The record company philosophy in America has always been: we'll give the public a choice of A, B or C but the menu stops here, and we'll decide that a band like Metallica will not be on the menu because they are not saleable.

"So we said, 'Fuck that'. Now, when they think they've got it all figured out again, we say, 'Fuck that', too. If it had been crap, we wouldn't have put it out. That was the deal. But it worked so well, we thought, 'Sure, why not?'"

As for receiving a Grammy for 'One', Lars remained healthily sceptical of the process by which the band found themselves the recipient of such a prestigious award. Having performed live at the 1989 Grammy Awards show and then stood by and watched incredulously as Jethro Tull, of all people, picked up that year's newly inaugurated award for Best Heavy Metal Act, his view was that, as he put it then, "If we release anything for the rest of the Nineties, every year we'll get a Grammy for it just because they fucked up that first year!

"Nobody's gonna want me to say that but that is where it's at. Listen man, we go into the studio and spend about 15 minutes – give or take a day – we spend the shortest visit we've ever had in the studio. But we go in, put down a cover version of a Queen song from 1973, OK, that appears on an Elektra compilation album and it's track 11 on side three, right? And it wins a Grammy over fully fledged albums by, like, Judas Priest and Megadeth?

"Don't you think that it has anything to do with, 'Gee, how can we rectify how we fucked up in 1989?' Nobody's gonna like me for saying that, but let's be honest."

BLACKENED

In contrast to the long, moody intros that had characterised both previous Metallica albums, 'Blackened' was straight out of its grimy little box and up and atcha.

Fading in on the screech of a magnificently over-wrought electric guitar, the drums arrive like a splatter-gun, the riff chewed up and spat out without ceremony over six-and-a-half minutes of angry hell. It takes half-a-dozen listens before you can really catch a hold of it and digest what's going on, and then you can't get it out of the worst corners of your mind.

It sounded like a song about the end of the world and in fact that's exactly what it was. As Lars explained at the time, "Lyrically, this one's about old Mother Earth and how she's not doing too well nowadays... how the whole environment that we're living in is slowly deteriorating into a shithole." It was not meant to be "a huge environmental statement," said Lars. "It's just a harsh look at what's going on around us."

No major changes there then...

...AND JUSTICE FOR ALL

Coming it at just under 10 minutes, the title track of the fourth Metallica album is one of the longest, most ambitious and, it has to be said, not entirely successful experiments of their adventurous career.

If the theme was grand – the death of the individual, the hopelessness of a government more interested in clinging to power than in changing people's lives for the better – the song itself was intended to be even grander.

As Lars acknowledged at the time: "It goes through some different shit along the way... It's pretty uppety-tempo for the most part, but it's a little different for us in that the main riff is centred around this weird drum beat that I came up with in the rehearsal studio one day. It's about the court systems in the US where it seems like no-one is even concerned with finding out the truth anymore. It's becoming more and more like a one-lawyer-versus-another-type situation, where the best (read: expensive) lawyer can alter justice in any way he wants."

Which is all fair enough. It's just that the message is rammed home so unrelentingly, it only takes a few listens to decide you don't want to sit through that again in a hurry, thanks very much.

A masterpiece of overstated, overblown, over-the-top-ness, this was a Cliff-less

Metallica struggling to prove that they were still the toughest new dicks on the block while trying nonetheless to say something larger than that. That they failed is to be forgiven; their courage in even attempting something like this to be commended. They would get it right next time.

EYE OF THE BEHOLDER

Welcome relief on the bristling back of a punchy meat-and-two-veg riff. Upbeat, pounding, James at his most clipped and aggrieved, Lars more or less sticking to the straightforward beat for once, Kirk combing the hair of the night with every deliberately inelegant swipe at his bruised guitar, only a couple of major shifts in pace to slow you down, quickly put right by a chorus that easily sends what's left of your poor brain spinning like a rat on a wheel.

'Eye Of The Beholder' should have been the first single from the album, but that would have been too easy. "Do you hear what I hear?" asks James, who sounds like he already knows the answer.

"We just never really considered it," Lars shrugged. "Right from the word go, we more or less decided that 'Harvester Of Sorrow' was the one that would be the single."

Asked for the story behind the song, as Lars said, "The lyrics to this one are pretty much self-explanatory. It's basically about people interfering with your way of thought, and how America is really maybe not as free as people think."

It was also about sounding good on the radio for the first time. Now there was an original thought...

ONE

In many people's eyes, this is the track that established Metallica as major league rock artists and not merely this year's happening metal band. Beyond the call of mere thrash, 'One' is a transcendent moment: one of the gloomiest, real-life tales ever told, it offered the bizarre spectacle of the band shedding crocodile tears over the plight of a disembodied life given a weird, strangled voice recognisable deep somewhere within the pit of our stomachs, in a place none of us want to be the next to visit, not now or ever.

"This was something that started out being about having no arms or legs, being deaf and blind, just like being a brain and nothing else. It's kind of scary and very fascinating all at once," explained Lars matter-of-factly. "Anyway, James had these ideas for lyrics and then [Metallica manager, Cliff] Bernstein suggested a book to me called *Johnny's Got A Gun* by a writer called Dalton Trumbo, which is about this guy who comes back from the war like that, so James got some input from that."

Indeed he did. The macabre story of an infantryman who steps on a land mine and wakes to gradually discover that he has lost everything – his limbs, his senses – except his mind, which is now cast adrift, trapped in its own grim and impossible reality. Wordless begging for death, 'One' was about living the ultimate nightmare; it's side-effect, to alter the circumstances surrounding Metallica forever. The irony: that it would make their own most extravagant post-bomb dreams come true.

THE SHORTEST STRAW

From the sublime...

"It deals with the whole blacklisting thing that took place in the Fifties," explained Lars at the time. "Where anyone whose view was a little out of the ordinary was immediately labelled as a potential threat to society. There were all these people in Hollywood whose views didn't fit in with the mainstream, and they were all shoved out of the entertainment industry because of their beliefs."

All very good. Or would be if the band sounded less stiff in the joints and more ready to rock. In their search for a rhythm abrasive enough to fit the subject, they finish up with a turgid, half-riff monstrosity that sounds far too

laboured-over and forced. A good idea that never really makes it past the drawing board.

Sadly, from there the rest of the ... *And Justice...* album begins a steady decline into all-out unlistenability. At least, that is, by comparison to the illicit confection of goodies their previous albums had all been.

 ### HARVESTER OF SORROW

A puzzling choice as the first legitimate Metallica single since 'Creeping Death' four years before, Lars remembered the track as "basic and instant". That is, he said, "compared to some of the other stuff on the album. It's a real heavy, bouncy, groovy type of thing. Plus, it's not too long by Metallica standards – it's only about five-and-a-half minutes long."

Maybe. But to the authors' ears this was bog-standard Metallica; full of swagger, certainly, but hardly startling by their own high standards. And as their first single on a major label, something of a major let down.

"Lyrically, this song is about someone who leads a very normal life, has a wife and three

kids, and all of a sudden one day, he just snaps and starts killing the people around him," Lars explained at the time.

It's a good yarn, all right, just not exactly rivetingly told. It had sounded underdeveloped and repetitive on the US 'Monsters Of Rock' tour, and it sounded no less so on the finished album.

Next...

 ### THE FRAYED ENDS OF INSANITY

Terrible title, yet, in truth, one of the more darkly impressive tracks on the album, once you got the hang of it. The trouble was, you needed the patience of a saint to unravel and appreciate this devil's music.

"It's a bit more musical and intricate than most of the other songs on the album," Lars explained. "It's got a pretty long musical middle part with a lot of changes and some pretty cool melodies. Over all, it's pretty much a mid-paced sort of thing, but it's really intricate and it might take a couple of listens before you can get into it."

You can say that again. Morbid, frankly depressing, you have to give the 'tune' (if that's the right word) credit for living up to its title, you just wouldn't want to wake up to it's Dracula face in the morning (and you certainly wouldn't want to go to bed with it at night). Creepsville.

TO LIVE IS TO DIE

At least, that's what you thought until you got to the seemingly boundless yawn-potential of 'To Live Is To Die'. "Our obligatory instrumental," joked Lars, the only person in the world who found it even mildly diverting. "Compared to our previous instrumentals, 'The Call Of Ktulu' and 'Orion', this one's a lot looser in some ways," he went on. "In that it's a bit more of a jam-type thing and not quite as square... "

Comprising several component parts that Cliff Burton had been tweaking around with before his death, perhaps in the band's eagerness to use something of Cliff's on this, their first album without him, blinded them to the number's otherwise pedestrian character.

"A lot of people might give us flak about this one because it features some stuff written by Cliff a few months before he was killed," said Lars. "But the truth of the matter is, these riffs were just so huge and so Metallica-sounding that we had to use them. We're certainly not trying to dwell on Cliff's death or anything like that – we're simply using the best ideas we had available, and this was one of them."

If you say so, chief...

DYER'S EVE

Mighty of riff but still disfiguringly awkward in both production and delivery, compared to a true album-closing masterpiece like 'Damage Inc.' which had shrouded the finale of *Master Of Puppets* in such a glowing sense of genuine awe, 'Dyer's Eve' was tolerable at best, deadly dull, at worst.

"It's basically about this kid who's been hidden from the real world by his parents the whole time he was growing up, and now that he's in the real world he can't cope with it and is contemplating suicide. It's basically a letter from the kid to his parents, asking them why they didn't expose him to the real world... "

Mmmm. Perhaps Metallica's problem on this album was that they themselves had been somewhat over-exposed to the world these past five years. The death of Cliff Burton had sapped them of their strength, and no matter how much they raged in his absence, or how many long faces Jason Newkid pulled from his side of the stage, on the whole the fourth Metallica album was a predictable disappointment, a gallant failure.

At the end of a very long day, a very strong sense of loss enshrouded the entire project. That it became, at that point, the most successful album of their career reflected more the status they had already achieved with the ground-breaking *Ride The Lightning* and *Master Of Puppets*, and less the dubious merits of this fraught and laboured recording.

Better – much better – would be expected next time.

METALLICA

Vertigo 510 022-1
Released August 1991

The key to the thinking behind the making of the fifth Metallica album could be detected in the choice of its title. Known simply as the *Metallica* album, or *Metallica V*, or even *The Black Album*, the mood was accessibility; the aim, chart action. This was an album that would be directed at all the people who had never bought a Metallica album before, but were now intrigued enough by the name to discover what all the fuss had been about for so long. As such, it did its job extremely well, becoming, in the long run, not just the most successful Metallica album of all time, but – according to *Billboard*, the US industry trade magazine – by 1995, it would also become the official biggest selling heavy metal album of all time, bar none!

It certainly took longer to record than any previous Metallica album. Holed up for six months at One On One studios in North Hollywood, once again Flemming Rasmussen was asked to wait silently in the wings while the band tried out a new producer. This time the choice was Bob Rock, the near-legendary Canadian producer who had provided the biggest hits of Bon Jovi, Motley Crüe and The Cult.

When co-author Wall interviewed Lars Ulrich at One On One halfway through the album, Wall began by commenting that bands only ever usually turned to Bob Rock to put them

in the charts, and wondered whether, by implication, that was what Metallica was attempting in its own weird way here?

"Yeah, that's a fair comment," Lars nodded thoughtfully. "But I look at it a little differently... We'd never really liked the mixing on *... and Justice ...* , *Master ...* or *... Lightning*. So we were thinking, who can we get in to do the mixing?

"We felt it was time to make a record with a huge, big, fat low-end and the best-sounding record like that in the last couple of years – not songs but sound – was the last Motley Crüe album. We really liked the really big fat sound on 'Dr. Feelgood'.

"Of course, we said, we're Metallica, no–one produces us, no-one fucks with our shit and tells us what to do. But slowly we thought maybe we should let our guard down and at least talk to the guy. Like, if the guy's name really is Bob Rock [it is], how bad can he be?" he chuckled.

"Then when we played him the stuff I could see his eyes light up. We'd built a little eight-track studio in my house and made some rough demos, just me on drums and James, not really everybody, just really rough."

Lars related how the first time the band played him a demo of 'Sad But True', "Bob was like, 'Wow, this could be the 'Kashmir' of the Nineties!' It was like, boom! From there, it was pretty much a done deal. We're just really excited in a way that I don't think we've been excited before. Bob says he thinks it shows we've got a lot of soul, or... What's another word for soul?"

Depth? Emotion?

"Yeah, we have a lot of emotions that we don't let out easily, 'cos we're very guarded as people. He says that he could see through that right away. He says that one of his things on this album was to try and let us take down our guard and let out the shit that's in there."

Lars admitted that it was also the band's attempt to seek the best path out of the thrash-rut ... *And Justice* ... had lost itself in.

"About half way through the 'Damaged Justice' tour, I was sitting there playing these nine-minute songs thinking, why am I sitting here worrying about how perfect these nine-minute songs have to be when we play stuff like 'Seek And Destroy' or 'For Whom The Bell Tolls' and it has a great fucking vibe?

"The way I look at it, Bob Rock brought out the best that Motley Crüe had to offer and made the best ever Motley record. The same with The Cult or Bon Jovi; if you listen to *Slippery When Wet*, there's no doubt Bob produced the best ever Bon Jovi album. And I think that's what he brought out in us on the last album: the best we had to offer at that time."

Even listening to some of the early playbacks, before most of the vocals had been completed, it was fairly plain to tell that this next album would represent a giant leap into commercialism. Not intrinsically a bad thing, of course, but always an interesting step to watch all former lords of the underground make.

"Well, I also think it's a combination of us getting pretty bored with the direction of the last three albums," he shrugged. "They were all different from each other, but they were all going in the same direction... you know, long songs, longer songs, even longer songs. Progressive, more progressive, even more progressive...

"And the reason for that, I think, is that, like, five minutes after I could play drums, Metallica was going, and the shit just rollercoasted. Suddenly we're making demos, then we're touring, making our first record. All of a sudden it was like, well, we have a record out but we really can't play. So I had to take drum lessons and Kirk's doing his Joe Satriani trip [Kirk used to take regular lessons from the San Francisco-based guitar ace]."

Wrapped in a plain black sleeve with the barely identifiable image of a serpent embossed on the front, untitled and understated (until you put the thing on!), *Metallica*, as it was known, was released worldwide on August 12, 1991 and shot straight into the US charts at number one, the first week of release.

To date, the fifth Metallica album has now sold in excess of eight million copies in the US alone, with a further seven million around the rest of the world.

"The heavy metal *Thriller*," as Def Leppard singer Joe Elliot once described it, and it is an apt depiction. "If no-one ever bought another Metallica album again, future generations would still be picking up on copies of *Metallica*," he went on, thoughtfully. "It's just a classic of its time. There's *Appetite For Destruction* by Guns N' Roses and there's *Metallica* by Metallica, and then there's the hundreds of bands that have tried to follow them with imitations and versions of their own. Amazing ... "

ENTER SANDMAN

The first thing that hits is that, Bob Rock or not, half the usual length maybe, this is still Metallica. Fearful as a widow's wail, bewitching as an unfull moon; it could be no other.

"It has these big fat guitar riffs," says Lars with relish. "But instead of after the second chorus steering into another fucking universe, they stay in the same one then go back into the chorus. Then we go to another universe on the next song."

Or to put it another way, with its huge singalong chorus and sensible stomping beat, it was the most direct thing Metallica had ever done and an obvious choice as first single off anybody's album. As a result, it raced to number five in the UK charts and to number 16 in the US.

Less issue-driven than previous albums, *Metallica* is their most f-u-n outing since

Kill 'Em All eight years before. There were still lots of topics that obsessed James' fevered imagination. But there were also a lot more personal reflections, too. 'Enter Sandman', the first single, was ostensibly about nightmares, but delved down deep into James' own childhood memories and his ever-present fear of the dark and what it might contain.

"That song had been on the fucking titles list for about six years," Lars smiled coyly when Wall spoke to him at One On One. "The way it works is, James and I sit with a big list of song titles and throw them at each other. We might pick one that will work with a specific guitar part. Others that don't catch straight away we just leave on there.

"I'd always looked at 'Enter Sandman' and thought, 'what the fuck does that mean?' Me being brought up in Denmark and not knowing about a lot of this shit, I didn't get it. Then James clued me in. The Sandman is like this children's villain – the Sandman who comes and rubs sand in your eyes if you don't go to sleep at night. So it's a fable and then Metallica turn it into a... "

Freddy Krueger?

"Nooo ... James has just given it a nice twist!" he laughed. "But it's this classic example of having something lingering around. People might say 'is that 'cos you can't come up with something new?' No, not at all.

"Six years ago I looked at 'Enter Sandman' and thought, 'Naw, let's write 'Metal Militia'... Metal all the way, you know?'" he squinted his eyes, then chuckled self–consciously.

SAD BUT TRUE

The track that Bob Rock described the first time he listened to the demo as "A 'Kashmir' for the Nineties," the main riff is certainly not a million B-sides away from the Led Zeppelin song from *Physical Graffiti*. Heavy as the cross, with a stunning landscaped sound that is part body-being-dragged-from-the-river, part atomic bulldozer.

Relentless as the plague, 'Sad But True' belongs in the same pantheon of Metalli-greats as 'Master Of Puppets' and 'Creeping Death'.

"It's about how different personalities in your mind make you do different things," Lars told Wall in 1991. "And how some of those things

Lars Ulrich with his father Torben in 1992

clash and how they fight to have control over you. From the mind of James Hetfield, you know what I mean?" he grinned evilly.

HOLIER THAN THOU

Straight all-out speed metal by any other name, but delivered with the punch of a state-of-the-art production. If Lars had forsaken some of his more delinquent fannying around on the drums for the march of the straight rock-steady beat, he had sacrificed none of his speed or dexterity. Indeed, he has never sounded more capable than on this album. And no more so readily than on 'Holier Than Thou'. A song built on drum-power if ever there was one.

THE UNFORGIVEN

"It's about how a lot of people go through their life without taking any initiative. A lot of people just follow in the footsteps of others. Their whole life is planned out for them, and there's certain people doing the planning and certain people doing the following."

WHEREVER I MAY ROAM

A rocker and, on the surface, a serious song about... what? Roaming around? Keeping on the move? Staying on your toes? What?

"Er, I think the genesis of that one actually goes back to the days when we were travelling around Europe sharing a bus with the roadies, the other bands on the bill, and whoever else managed to get on board between gigs," Lars recalled with a wry smile.

"In order to get by, you often had to look the other way and just ignore what was going on. You had to be very like, 'Oh, well, whatever', you know?"

Does he mean groupies? Drugs? Drunken parties? Or just other people's dirty laundry?

"Er, I mean everything!" he chirped merrily, the memories still warm in his back pocket.

DON'T TREAD ON ME

A brutal, riff-heavy piece of work that leaps straight over the borders of macho and into the goggle-eyed realms of the truly bullyful, 'Don't Tread On Me' was understandably misread at the time as a jingoistic call-to-arms for stars-and-stripes wavers everywhere.

But, as Lars explained: "After the put-downs and cynicism of so much of the material on ... And Justice For All and Master Of Puppets, you know, where we really did attack a lot of what passes for good old-fashioned American virtue but is in actual fact a crock of shit, the irony was that the success those albums brought us meant we got to really travel the world and have a look around for ourselves and see what was out there.

"And the truth is, how James talked about it when he wrote the songs anyway, was that, if you're an American, there really is no place like home. You know, no matter how fucked or corrupt our administration may be, or how many dirty deeds go on that we know nothing about, America, for us, is still the most pleasant, comfortable and exciting place in the world! It really is!

"So I guess, after putting the place down so much, James just figured he'd write something from the opposite point of view. Like, no place is all bad, like no place is all good. James just thinks America has more of the good in it than any place else right now." So there.

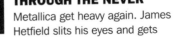

THROUGH THE NEVER

Metallica get heavy again. James Hetfield slits his eyes and gets mean. And the band come up with one of the best all out thrashers on an album largely devoted to disguising such pug-origins.

What was it about? "Search me," Lars joked at the time. "I think James is still trying to come up with the answer to that one. I think it's about the urge to break on through to... a different world."

And did he make it? "I don't know, but we had a great fucking time trying!"

NOTHING ELSE MATTERS

Cushioned by a 40-piece orchestra, soothed by whispering cellos and lulled into daydreams by the swish of violins, 'Nothing Else Matters' was the song that nobody, least of all James Hetfield, would have thought possible back in the now-gone days of 'Whiplash' and 'The Four Horsemen': a tender love song.

It is a rare glimpse into the hidden romanticism of a man not best-known for his more caring side. As Hetfield tried to explain at the time: "That song was just me and my guitar on the road. It came together somewhere in Canada, I think. I just sat in my room working on this thing. It was a personal thing. I played it for myself. But I played it for Lars and he listened and said, 'Man, that's pretty cool'. And I thought, 'Yeah, it is'.

"It's not a safe song, it takes some nerve for us to do," he confessed. "We're not supposed to do something like that. Well, who said we couldn't, you know?"

'Nothing Else Matters' would also provide Metallica with their second hit single from the album. Metallica have a hit with a love song.

OF WOLF AND MAN

The band get their heavy metal asses back into gear and head for their speed roots for this next one. In truth, they had by this time left behind this sort of thing: ludicrously fast with an even more ludicrous title. But 'fun' was their watchword with this one and that's what they sound like they're having.

With Bob Rock giving the band a much fuller, resonant sound, the panic in Hetfield's vocals cut right through to the bone – his voracious tone the perfect counterpoint to the frenetic, driving rhythms of Ulrich and Newsted, the latter sounding as loaded and cocksure as he had sounded oblique and lost on the previous album.

One up for the diehards.

THE GOD THAT FAILED

Moulded, like 'Dyer's Eve' from ... *And Justice ...*, by the psychological turmoil of James Hetfield's adolescence, dealing with an angry and bitter world he simply never knew existed because of the cloistered upbringing his strict Christian Science parents had imposed upon him.

At the time, Lars was quick to deflect attention away from the personal into the general. "'The Unforgiven'," he said, was about "this thing that's going on in America. This kind of religion thing where they don't believe in medicine. So if their kids get some heavy illness it's like, 'Please God, heal this sick child' and three days later the child is dead. The courts are going after these people now and charging them with murder. But it's not necessarily against or for. It just tells a story..."

But it was clear to those who knew him well that James had embarked on a new era in his

lyric-writing. He had always been blunt and opinionated. Now he was seasoning the flow with new strands of sensitivity and honesty he had never dared contemplate before.

"It's stirring up a lot of shit over here," Lars said, and you could see why. 'The Unforgiven' addressed that most American of subjects: how my mom and dad fucked me up. Only this time it wasn't because of incest or child-beating or drug and alcohol abuse; it was because of something called religion. One of the 'new American' religions at that.

Ouch.

MY FRIEND OF MISERY

A number full of melodic intent, '... Misery' has an approach redolent of Black Sabbath in their Seventies-prime. Another ballad, though not in the sugared style of 'Nothing Else...'. This was doleful and black; not something that would stand the daylight of mainstream radio, James singing his chops off. No screaming, no growling, just plain wailing at the moon.

It should be interesting to hear this one in the years to come. Could this be another way forward for the band? From thrash-metal to rose-petal (with thorns) in just five albums?

Who knows? But if any track showcases James Hetfield's new-found ability to sing beautiful songs, this is it.

THE STRUGGLE WITHIN

Most bands would have chosen to end this album by virtually burning up on re-entry; after the experiments and showcasing, time for a nice 'n' nasty bit of schlock and roll, if you please, maestro!

But no. True to that perverse spirit which has saved them from being forever pigeonholed as either 'heavy' or 'thrash' metal (unlike nearly all their contemporaries, from Megadeth to Anthrax and Slayer, all of whom have remained in the metal ghetto), Metallica decided to end their most chart-friendly album yet with a mid-tempo number that still

displayed more power and bravura than most metal bands manage in a whole album's worth of bass-bin burners.

Kirk Hammett is in his element, firing out the powder-blue lines as Lars' sonically booming kit is virtually set ablaze, but once again none of the band's brashness or clear-sighted sense of power is allowed to overshadow a magnificent awareness of melody and structure.

Bob Rock had inspired a new respect for songs per se in the band. He showed them how you don't have to overwhelm to impress. 'The Struggle Within' says as much. It was a fittingly confident climax to a milestone record.

LIVE SHIT!
BINGE AND PURGE

Vertigo 518 726-2 –
November 1993

Long before they had scaled the heights of the world's charts, Metallica had decided never to do things by halves, quarters or any other fraction, for that matter. They have made it their rule that when they go for a target, they throw in everything, including the kitchen sink – and usually it works wonders!

Thus during the summer of 1993, the band were preparing to unleash not just a live album, not just a live video, not just a combination thereof, but a whole suitcase full of the stuff! Commemorative in appeal, outlandish in its ambition, *Live Shit! Binge And Purge* was destined to become the most sought after and most little-owned of all Metallica albums. Something to please everybody.

The clamour for a live Metallica album had been deafening for a long time. Their reputation built on the legend of the band's uncompromising live performances, illegal bootlegs recordings had flourished as under-the-counter live Metallica albums from day one.

Their most ardent fans hoped that the band would one day officially put out a vintage live set drawn from the Cliff Burton years – but Metallica themselves felt that they had answered that inevitable call with the release of their historic *The $19.99 Home Vid – Cliff 'Em All* docu-video in 1988. There was no going back now. And in late 1992, they unveiled a special Christmas present for their fans with the release of a monstrous two-volume video titled *A Year And A Half In The Life Of Metallica/*

A Year And A Half In The Life Of Metallica Continued which documented the making of the *Metallica* album in great visual detail (warts 'n' all) and also some of the subsequent touring process.

They'd even unleashed the *Metallican* in June 1993, which consisted of an 8" x 6" metallic can containing a 'Nowhere Else To Roam' T-shirt, a gold CD version of the *Metallica* album, a booklet signed by the band and the three-track *Outrageous* video, featuring live versions of the Anti-Nowhere League's 'So What', and Diamond Head's 'Helpless' and 'Am I Evil'. But all this was as nought as compared to what was coming next.

By June 1993, as Metallica confirmed their headlining date at the Milton Keynes Bowl – on a bill also featuring Megadeth, The Almighty and a reformed Diamond Head – they also announced the first tentative details of this live release.

At this point it seemed that it would be simply a live CD and an accompanying video. The latter had apparently been filmed in San Diego, California, the previous year and the video would actually present the show in its entirety, plus an additional 30 minutes of footage culled from a date in Seattle during 1989 on the tour to promote *... And Justice For All*.

In the meantime, the album itself would feature an entire show from Mexico City recorded the previous February. Thus fans were going to be treated to some six hours-plus of hard music and heavy visuals.

"It's Metallica doing a clean sweep of the attic," announced Lars at the time. "We've got all this stuff lying around. We thought, 'Instead of just doing a live album, what can we do that's a pretty cool package?' If you want it, you get everything, about six or seven hours of Metallica! One whole show on video and one on album. It'll show how the tour evolved.

"We sat down and listened to the San Diego stuff and thought, 'We sucked at the beginning of this tour, maybe we should record some stuff from later on when we started playing better'. We don't have anything to hide. People can see how a band evolves in a year-and-a-half."

The album was due to be mixed in San Francisco and was to serve as a stop-gap for Metallica fans, because come July 4, 1993 (when the lengthy world tour was supposed to finish), the plan was... well, that there would be no plans for the band for some while. They intended to take a long break from anything to do with rock'n'roll. It could be at least three years before anything new was to appear.

Of course, knowing Metallica things would not be as simple as they seemed in June. Within a couple of months, the proposed simultaneous release of a 'mere' live album and CD had been grandiosely altered. Stand by for a mega-mega Metallica box set!

By the end of October, *Live Shit! Binge And Purge* was being announced. This was to be an unbelievable package containing two three-hour videos, a triple CD, a 72-page booklet, a special commemorative pass that would 'allow' the holder into the infamous 'Snake Pit' that was situated at the front of the stage at every Metallica show in the world tour, and a stencil of the Metallica 'skull' logo, known colloquially as 'The Scary Guy'! All of this was to be housed in a specially constructed flight case, albeit one made from cardboard as opposed to metal.

It was set fair to be a massive release. *Live Shit...* would be limited to just 10,000 sets in the UK and would retail at £75, with the release confirmed as November 23. Parents across the world quaked in their Santa outfits as the inevitable occurred: "Can I have the new Metallica album for Christmas?" AAARRRGGGHHH!!!!

But this was something aimed fair and square at true Metallica fanatics, not those who had only just picked up on the band because they'd had some chart success. "If we put these things out separately over the years, it would cost the same amount of money, maybe more," was Hetfield's rehearsed riposte when the heavy price was continually called into question.

Lars defended the release thus: "Looking around and seeing what bands have done in terms of putting stuff out – single videos, double videos, a single CD, a double CD – I feel that's ripping people off. What we're doing here is saying, 'Here it is, take it or leave it.'"

Lars also put the blame for the high cost of the set firmly down to trying to cover costs. "Our management did a survey and discovered that this is the most expensive packaging anybody has ever put together. You've got everything in there: nine hours of music, a 72-page booklet, backstage passes, stencil, keys to our house... so just take it or leave it!"

So, what exactly did this remarkable offer consist of? Well, the videos (two of 'em) were both complete shows. The first was filmed in Seattle during 1989 on the ...And Justice For All stretch. The second was shot in San Diego on the 'Wherever...' trek.

As for the audio accompaniment, this was recorded in Mexico City over a five-night period, whilst the booklet included loads of photos taken by official snapper Ross 'The Master' Halfin that had never previously been seen, as well as detailed faxes and itineraries that give their own insight into the bizarre machinations of Metallica on the road.

"It really all started out with us only wanting to document the shows we did on the 'Wherever...' tour and just add in a bonus live CD," explained Lars at the time. "So we shot two gigs in San Diego at the beginning of the tour (using a full 10-camera crew). The plan then was to use this footage, and just throw in some bonus stuff from two Seattle gigs in '89 (again these were filmed with a similar arsenal of cameras)."

But as the time came around for the band to start winding their way through the huge mound of video footage and pick what they wanted to use, they were 15 months into their present world tour.

"When we finally sat down and listened to the San Diego stuff, the set list had changed so much and we were playing a lot better as well," said Lars. "So, we decided to document some more stuff."

And that's when the idea occurred to all and sundry to add in a bonus CD. "We were sitting there facing the fact that we had five nights in Mexico City and the idea came up to record these shows just on audio."

Then the band tackled the Seattle footage. Originally, the plan had been just to pick those tracks performed in Seattle that were no longer a part of their live set (these being 'The Thing That Should Not Be', 'Master Of Puppets', '...And Justice For All' and a cover of the Budgie standard 'Breadfan'). But having played back the whole gig, somebody came up with the bright notion of releasing it in its entirety!

"We'd actually talked about hanging on to the Seattle stuff and putting it out about 10 years further on down the line," admitted James. "That way it would be, 'Wow, here's some vintage crap that's never been seen and, wow, it's on proper film'. But as we started to watch it, we found that it was pretty alright stuff, and we agreed just to get it all out now so it doesn't look really out of place later."

For the booklet, Lars and James sifted through piles of faxes to find suitably silly and fun stuff to share with the fans. And, as is usual in the Metallicamp, it was this duo who were overseeing every aspect of the packaging, whilst Hammett and

Newsted were on the periphery of the whole situation.

Upon its release, *Live Shit!...* received rave reviews from the media. Mike Peake in *Kerrang!* tagged it as "brilliant... It contains some of the finest, meatiest live material ever released in hard rock, and is quite possibly Metallica's finest hour."

THE GOOD, THE BAD & THE UGLY

It's Mexico. It's The Sports Palace in Mexico City. It's late February (25-27). It's early March (1-2) 1993. It's METALLICA LIVE!!!

And while 'The Good, the Bad & The Ugly' is the taped intro – taken from the classic spaghetti western of the sane title and composed by Ennio Morricone – this has become such a major part of the Metallica legend that it had to be included.

This is a glorious orchestral extravaganza. The perfect way to rouse the crows. The lights dip, the stirring tones raise the temperature, the band prepare for their entrance. In fact, Morricone's theme is metal by deed and implication, proving you don't need electric guitars, drums and amplifiers to make a monster sound.

ENTER SANDMAN

And so, straight into the action. As the taped intro faded, the band struck up with the unmistakable opening chords to the classic 'Enter Sandman'. The rolling, dark rhythm struts out through the PA system, raising the crowd to a point of virtual hysteria.

This version was performed at a slightly brisker pace than the original studio rendition, but then that's inevitable. You can almost feel the overwhelming adrenalin rush coursing through Metallica's veins as they soak themselves in the radiant sweat and total ferment of the massive crowd. And at a greater velocity than in the studio, this massive song sounds even more convincing and spectacular.

James' vocals aren't for the faint-hearted. He snarled and bellowed as if about to leap into a pit of werewolves. This was a metal band stripped down to their soul, cutting deep to the bone. No quarter asked. None given.

Lars speeds up and slows down as he gamely attempts to fit the right meter for his drum fills. But all this proves is that the live tapes have hardly been touched in the studio, as is so often the case with live releases. With Metallica what you got on the night is what you got here. Anyone out in Mexico City for this series of shows would probably agree that here is the band in their natural state of euphoric, ectoplasmic, ear-splitting epic finery.

CREEPING DEATH

No Metallica show would ever be complete without this particular raging torrent of anthemic thrash in the set. And here it sounded as dynamic and formidable as it ever has. Maybe it was the heated atmosphere of the Mexican cauldron, but there was something searing and nasty about this rendition.

Metallica might have moved away from their thrash roots and into a more mainstream style and sound, but they could still get down into the gutter and release pent-up fury with the best of 'em.

What always stood out with 'Creeping Death' live was the manner in which Metallica audiences of any size and shape gleefully leapt in to chant along those pleasant words 'DIE, DIE, DIE'! – hell's choir indeed.

This particular singalong rendering was among the most frenetic and evil one could wish to hear. It literally jumps out of the speakers. Egged on by a veritably crazed Hetfield, the song came to life as it never could in a studio. And even if again there are signs of the band failing to keep perfect time, what did it matter? This was the live arena and such things as perfect tempo are irrelevant.

HARVESTER OF SORROW

Probably the best track from ...*And Justice For All* given a slightly different treatment onstage. To hear the band getting into middle gear for this song is a joy to behold. After the frenetic opening, something was needed to calm down the

atmosphere just a tad, and this mid-pocket mayhemic marvel is just the ticket.

Newsted's steadily puffing bass provided a solid foundation on which the band could build a steadily mounting attack. And, while in the studio this particular track suffered somewhat from the album's overtly dry production technique, onstage there was nothing at all dry and distant about the way in which they threw themselves into the song. It sounded mature, balanced, but also brimming with testosterone.

WELCOME HOME (SANITARIUM)

When this first appeared on the *Master Of Puppets* album it was hailed as a radical departure for Metallica. A lengthy, intelligent exposition that proved they were leaving their contemporaries flailing, by the time they came to release this version live, it represented a crucial part of the Metallihistory. The irony is that it didn't really work quite as well live, because the individual musicians just didn't seem to be able to adjust well enough to fit in with the demands of the song.

Hammett's guitar parts were too ragged. Ulrich's drum fills were frighteningly inept, and Newsted's bass just doesn't have the full ripeness of his predecessor.

Yet, forged on by Hetfield's impassioned vocal display, this track overcame all disabilities to rise triumphantly from the mire. It still sent shivers down the spine and proved itself to be a vital ingredient of the live set. No Metallica performance would be complete with it.

SAD BUT TRUE

Leading on from the relative delicacy of 'Welcome Home...' came the mid-tempo punch of 'Sad But True', another winner from the *Metallica* album. There is a feeling of dark resignation about the number when heard in its studio context, but again this is burnt away when the band took it to the stage.

'Sad But True' is a clear mid-set highlight here, acting as a bridge between what had been to some extent a surprising downbeat opening salvo and the upcoming sonic flamboyance to come.

With Hetfield rasping at his peak, the song no longer seemed grounded in self-reflection, but began to exist in its own right as something of a Metallica classic. In the wash of top-notch material that graced the *Metallica* album, this song is one easy to forget. Not onstage, though. A genuine high spot of the show.

OF WOLF AND MAN

To most Metallica fans this is one song that probably remains consigned to obscurity. When the *Metallica* record is discussed this number would very rarely come to the fore. It had been forgotten. So, it came as something of a surprise when the band chose to perform it live. But then the element of surprise is what makes Metallica somewhat different to run-of-the-mill platinum acts.

'Of Wolf And Man' wasn't an obvious number to play live. It is a difficult track to work simply because it has little for the fans to hold onto. It's a slightly disparate number that provides for a few intricate chord changes, but Metallica acquitted themselves well to the task and made it work by sheer force of will, adrenalin and momentum.

GUITAR DOODLE

Metallica have always messed around live. Sometimes they've played the opening chords from well-known songs such as Iron Maiden's 'Run To The Hills' or Black Sabbath's 'Paranoid'. On other occasions, it has just meant a little instrumental interplay and nonsense. It's done to counter the threat of monotony and boredom that can come from playing the same set every night.

On this live recording, Hammett and Hetfield just pratted around for a brief period, in reality doing nothing more than tuning up. But it did the trick of allowing the band to catch their breath and prepare to dive straight into the next assault, which was...

THE UNFORGIVEN

One of the most celebrated cuts from *Metallica*, this was a majestic number full of Morricone-style nuances and intricacies. It's not truly a metal song, being more, much more, than that.

But what works on record didn't necessarily work on stage. And this frankly did not. The problem was that the grand sweep of the music on record wasn't allowed to come through onstage and what we're left with was a number that paled by comparison to what had gone before.

The band themselves seemed out of sorts with the serious demands of this song on the night in question, and the result was sadly almost a travesty.

...AND JUSTICE FOR ALL

The title track of that fourth album – and after 'The Unforgiven' this came as something of a breath of fresh air. Very long – in the studio, some might say it was overlong – the number could have been an unmitigated disaster when transferred to the stage. But the band seemed more in tune with this cut than 'The Unforgiven'.

There are just some nights when certain songs work, while on others they don't. This evening proved to be an example of the former as far as this sprawling number was concerned. The band almost seemed to relish the challenge provided by giving ...*And Justice For All* fair treatment. Result: quite a magnificent representation.

BASS SOLO/GUITAR SOLO

The fine art of soloing has always been a tradition of heavy metal shows. Usually, they're meandering doodles that do nothing save give the rest of the band a welcome breather. Very few solos ever stand out.

Metallica gave Cliff Burton his own solo spot simply as a way of sending up the whole notion. His solo was so off-the-wall that it became an essential ingredient for any Metallica gig. But when he died, the band made the foolhardy mistake of allowing his successor Jason Newsted his own spot. The cruel truth was that Newsted only showed up his own inadequacies, as well as proving what a monumentally talented man Burton had been.

Thus his solo, by the time this tour came around, was forgettable doodling nonsense, representing everything Metallica claimed to hate and loathe in the genre. It was horrible, in fact – too long, laborious and boring.

As far as Hammett's guitar solo was concerned, again it went against the grain of Metalli-legend. The band had always stood against the idea of the guitar hero. Yet, as their set became increasingly lengthy (stretching to nearly three hours by this time), there was a need for a guitar solo to help break up the set – and give the others a breather. But to put it in straight after Newsted's solo was poor timing. It made for agitation, unease and boredom in the crowd. Moreover, the solo itself was ill-conceived in construction and execution.

In fact, the dreaded combination of these solos was so mind-numbingly dull that one has to wonder whether they were included to make the crowd more appreciative of what came next. So, sly psychology or a joke that went wrong? It's up to the individual listener.

THROUGH THE NEVER

Yet another surprising choice from the *Metallica* album, this number eased the whole band back into gear after they'd been stalling via those solos. Once more, Metallica showed an ability to surprise and shock with their live interpretation of a song most would never have expected in a live set.

Not exactly a highlight of the show, but coming after those solos it was a real boon.

FOR WHOM THE BELL TOLLS

And so the crowd is wound up another notch by the introduction of an all-time favourite. By now, Metallica were back in their stride, on familiar territory and ready to burn.

'For Whom The Bell Tolls' has been part of their live set since the 'Ride The Lightning' tour. It's one of those numbers the band could never leave out – although they'll probably contrive to do so one day just to surprise us all!

This version was as good as any they've ever done. There was never any doubt that it was gonna take the roof right off the place – and it does. Listening to Hetfield winding the crowd up to fever pitch once more was a sheer joy to behold – a master at work!

FADE TO BLACK

The other epic from *Ride The Lightning* thrown in to maintain the momentum of an era captured to perfection during this point in the set. Many bands lose sight of what made them popular in the first place once they break big, but not Metallica. They still had the ability to play the old stuff with that embryonic sense of fervour and passion.

The sound quality on this track was especially impressive, allowing full separation between instruments yet moulding them together into a mesh of mosh-pit mayhem. Such is its spontaneity, this song sounds as if it's being played for the first time.

MASTER OF PUPPETS

The title track from that third album came riding over the horizon to an ecstatic reception. It is a continual source of amazement just how many Metallica songs are recognisable after just a couple of chords – this is one of 'em.

Hammett is at his best here, dropped notes notwithstanding. It didn't matter how many mistakes one can hear, the plain fact was that the overall drive and bullishness of the song allowed it to career virtually on the edge of being out of control – without actually going over the metaphorical cliff. Follow that! OK, let's try...

SEEK AND DESTROY

Another bracing number that called for a singalong-a-chorus, 'Seek And Destroy' might be something of a gumby anthem that has almost become a parody in

the 15 years since it was written, but live it was a sure fire hit.

Crowds love to be wound up and let loose. They love to have the chance to shake their heads in a furious onslaught of dandruff and sweat. And nothing in the Metallica set this night got a better response than this old chestnut. You can shout... you can bellow... you can roar... you can stomp your feet or clap your hands. This is a song that doesn't allow for subtlety – and didn't get any tonight from either band or crowd. Little else need be said. It's a roller coaster ride of brutal machismo. Nobody outside of the metal circle will ever understand the value of a song like this – but who cares?!

WHIPLASH

One anthem fades, another raises its ugly head. 'Whiplash' is always guaranteed to shake any foreign bodies out of a fan's system. It's a no-holds barred, flame-throwing opera of sonic mutilation and jack-boot creativity.

There were tens of thousands of fans that night banging those heads that would not bang. The very swish of the air comes across on the album as a tidal wave of energy. It was Metallica mania taken to fresh heights. There is probably not another two-song combination anywhere in metal so certain to provide a double-barrel explosion through your chest.

And the glee with which Metallica attacked this number was almost obscene. Love it!

NOTHING ELSE MATTERS

Sometimes one has to take the foot off the accelerator. If Metallica had attempted to maintain the furious pace they were now setting, chances are that they'd have shaken a few heads loose – and provided the basis for several thousand law suits.

So, the band braked hard and opened up the *Metallica* coffers once again – finding a solid-gold winner in the gentle (well, by comparison anyway) 'Nothing Else Matters'. A chance for Hetfield to sing (very well), for the band to slam down hard and pull the crowd down through the gears (successfully) and for melody to triumph over muscle (impressively).

WHEREVER I MAY ROAM

The anthem of the tour. The song that sums up the band's philosophy. The slow, brooding monstrosity from the *Metallica* album came to life onstage, even if in the studio it was somewhat stifled by a surfeit of effects and technology.

Coming as it did right after 'Nothing Else Matters' it was somewhat of a winner. There was an unusual feeling of coupling on this live album. The band would play two out-and-out stompers followed by two less speedy items, followed by an increase in pace, and so on. It was a tactic that worked rather well.

AM I EVIL

The slow-burning intro was unmistakable. The climactic Hammer horror crescendo that led straight into the multi-fretboard frenzy from Kirk Hammett. Here comes that Diamond Head cover again, and it's biting down hard!

'Am I Evil' has been a major part of the Metallica live set for as long as most people can recall. They've made it their own, by dint of not so much reinterpreting it as realigning it. A song that could have been written by them – or for them – the confident, strident manner in which the band attacked it here amply underscored the fact that, although 'Am I Evil' might have been written in Stourbridge, it had now been hijacked by the ultimate 'Metal Militia'. Sorry, boys.

LAST CARESS

From a Diamond Head cover to one from The Misfits. It's fair to say that without the patronage of Metallica in general, and Hetfield in particular, The Misfits would have been consigned to the musical equivalent of the dumper. Metallica not only brought The Misfits into the public domain, but gave band mainman Glenn Danzig the opportunity to establish his own niche.

'Last Caress' first appeared on the covers EP *The $5.98 EP: Garage Days Re-revisited*. Subsequently it was spasmodically performed live by the band. Here it came across as something of a goth-punk anthem given a sheer metal extirpation. It worked.

ONE

The big hit that changed many people's attitudes towards the band by proving they could break into the charts without going mainstream.

The intelligence and thought that went into writing the number, though, was irrelevant once it took on a live angle. It was a fired-up classic that had real melodic sensibility. And on this night, Metallica did it proud. Nary a sign of tiredness in the presentation or performance. And when you hear how the band skip through it, 'One' really does sound like a traditional heavy metal song with no connection to the thrash genre they were supposedly leading into a new era. If any song proved Metallica's allegiance to tried and trusted values, here it was.

SO WHAT

The Anti-Nowhere League's nihilistic shock-proof anthem given an overhaul by Metallica. This appeared in studio form on the Japanese version of the *Metallica* album, and was now given a feisty airing live by the band. Actually, nothing in the set sounded quite so basic, quite so furious, quite so manic as this number. But Hetfield seemed to almost relish the challenge, whilst the rest of the band actually had little trouble in keeping up the necessary pace.

BATTERY

Pounding the world like a battering ram, forging the furnace for the final grand slam, here came Metallica riding high on the hog and raiding their own catalogue for something suitably crazed to follow up from 'So What' They found it, in the form of this *Master Of Puppets* hooligan toon.

Even after all these years, the boys could still blow up a storm on this number and the literally breathless pace they set here would even bring Linford Christie to his knees. How, after more than two-and-a-half hours

onstage, the fearsome foursome were still able to burst blood vessels remains one of the great mysteries of humanity!

THE FOUR HORSEMEN

The end is in sight. The chequered flag awaited as the band turned to the tried and trusted apocalyptic raid to turn everything up a further notch. Honestly, one had to stand back in admiration at the way in which the band could make even this number – one they'd been performing live for many, many years by this juncture – heave with renewed zeal and zest.

MOTORBREATH

One more from the vault, 'Motorbreath' would have been the perfect way for Metallica to round off the evening's entertainment – except that it was to be no more than the penultimate crack this time around.

But the band rallied around the old flag in fine form and gave this particular pensionable tune a rousing send-off, with Ulrich hammering his kit as if trying to wreak some kind of Valkyric havoc.

STONE COLD CRAZY

Yes, the Queen classic which Metallica first recorded for the *Rubaiyat* album in 1990, a 39-track collection released to celebrate Elektra's 40th anniversary which consisted of current bands on the label covering songs by others signed to the company. Now, it brought everything in Mexico City to a suitably rousing finale.

As with every cover they've attempted, Metallica had the ability to make this number their own. And this they achieved in no uncertain terms. A fitting – if rather strange – way in which to end this essentially supreme 177-minute 18-second performance, which for completists, contained 11 uses of the word 'shit' and no less than 66 of the word 'fuck'!

LOAD

**Vertigo 532 618-2 –
June 1996**

When you've sold nine million copies of an album in the States and a further five or six million worldwide you have a problem... what next?

Metallica faced this situation in 1995, as they prepared to follow-up *Metallica*, the album that transformed the San Francisco cult heroes into a metal phenomenon and the most successful band of that genre ever.

Strangely, instead of feeling any pressure, the challenge of coming up with something at least the equal of their fifth album actually relaxed the band. As Lars Ulrich said in the midst of the recording process: "As far as I'm concerned, we haven't recorded for five years and suddenly we're in the thick of it. It's like going through a crash barrier. And we survived that one moment of 'starting recording' without the world falling in on us. Since then, we've looked through the curtain at the other side and seen that things are actually pretty cool."

Another reason for this almost laid-back attitude might have been that the band chose to record right on their own doorstep. For the first time, they used a studio close to their home base in San Francisco (The Plant in Sausalito, North California), which meant that they didn't have to up roots and relocate to a temporary, alien environment for any length of time.

Said Lars: "Because we're at home – and not going somewhere else and uprooting camp – is maybe part of the reason recording really wasn't that big a deal. The whole air is very positive."

"Being at home is definitely a lot more relaxed," added James Hetfield. "We didn't know how it would work – you either can't concentrate as much, or you're relaxed – but it's worked out pretty good. We've eased into it pretty well."

Moreover, their relationship with producer Bob Rock had developed from one of close-cropped and mutual strangeness into a more committed situation. Commented Lars: "The confidence in Bob is way higher than it was last time. We made the whole of the last record with him, and as a result, this time around he's completely clued in. Our relationship with him is a lot more grounded now. So, it's a little easier for us to let go a bit, and that also helps to make things more relaxed. Nobody's up anyone's ass; we're not breathing down everybody's backs. Because the relationship with Bob is a lot looser this time, the songs are also a lot looser. Everybody's getting on well.

"One thing we're consciously doing is taking weekends off. We're trying not to kill ourselves to get the album done in a certain amount of time. Every record we've ever made, we've pushed ourselves to the point where it affected our relationship and we've all started hating each other. This time we're making sure that it's loose enough never to get to that point."

One significant development as the summer of 1995 unfurled was that the four members seemed at ease with their specific roles within the band, as Kirk Hammett explained. "There's a comfort and solidarity to everything we're doing in the studio. We're all in this together, and we're all very clear of our roles on this album.

"Nowadays, I think Lars and James are also more comfortable with me throwing ideas towards the songs. We all write music and the best parts are cherry picked. But now, more than ever before, the guys are open to what I write – which in itself gives me more confidence in suggesting things about arrangements or adding creative flourishes.

"Lars and James always have a certain vision as to how a song should go. Sometimes that vision is very, very obvious – other times it isn't so obvious to me. But now it's like a musical think tank, with everyone sitting around a table and throwing ideas around."

Pausing only to make a surprise headlining visit to the Castle Donington 'Monsters Of Rock' festival in the UK on August 26 (where the band also débuted two songs set for inclusion on the new album, although the titles of both were still to be set in stone), the band worked steadily, relocating to Right Track Studios in New York to finish off the recording during March and April of 1996. And during late May the first fruit of their labour was released in the UK, the single 'Until It Sleeps', which made a huge dent on the Top 5, accompanied not only by a rather surreal, quasi-religious video, but also by the first sign of a change in Metallica's image, as the band cut off their hair and went for a much more contemporary image.

"Hair's become so fucking useless to us," claimed Hetfield. "This is the shortest my hair has been since I was born."

On June 3, the new album finally hit the shops. Titled *Load* it swept to the top of the charts in most countries around the world, including Britain and the States. Indeed, the album quickly passed the gold standard of 100,000 copies in the UK, while in America *Load* spent its first four weeks of release occupying the top slot – a remarkable achievement even by Metallica's own remarkable standards. And this was before they hit the road in support of the record!

There was some controversy over the album cover. Titled *Semen And Blood 3*, it was ostensibly a painting by controversial European artist Andres Serrano. But some suggested that Metallica had recreated this piece of artwork by using Hammett's semen, something the amused guitarist denied. "It's not true! The photo we've used is part of a series done by Serrano with different mixes of blood and semen. I saw the artwork in a book at the San Francisco Museum Of Modern Art and I was so intrigued that I told the rest of the band we should use it for the album cover. Lars immediately agreed, as did James, but Jason didn't fancy the idea quite as much as the others, but we won him over."

Metallica also caused a few eyebrows to be raised at the sheer length of *Load*. At 78 minutes 59 seconds it was the longest album ever to be put on one CD. Once again, Metallica were giving value for money.

Musically, it was a reaffirmation that the band were always striving to set new standards. This was the sound the late Nineties redefined and siphoned through the Metallica perspective. "Twelve years ago, when we started opening up on the *Ride The Lightning* album with songs like 'Fade To Black', a lot of people said, 'What the fuck is this all about?' And we said, 'We don't want to be stuck doing one thing'," attested Lars. "I know *Load* is different, but I also know it's really fucking strong Metallica."

Added Jason Newsted: "If anything, the experimentation level here is higher than ever before. The guitars and bass are definitely looser. For the first time, we did what 98 per cent of other bands do – put the bass down right on the drums, and then the guitar after that. Kirk also played rhythm guitar for the first time. That added a lot to the character of the album. What would I say about *Load*? Well, the last album was great, but this one is a bit more real."

AIN'T MY BITCH

Co-written by Hetfield and Ulrich, this song not only opens up the *Load* album, but sets the tone for what is to follow. Based on a neatly clipped semi-blues riff from Hammett, the song pours all over the stereo, with an almost languorous, viscous liquidity. The by-word throughout the album is most definitely 'relaxed', a term constantly on the lips of the band members themselves when they spoke about the vibe in the studio, and 'Ain't My Bitch' supplies the fuel to prove this definition.

This is a blues-metal work-out that has much in common with Motörhead, one of Metallica's primary – and enduring – influences. There is a distinct late Nineties gait to the song, proving that Metallica were out to do something very different while remaining true to themselves, their traditions and their fans. And Hammett at once displays an increased repertoire by producing an impressive slide guitar solo, something he would never have attempted, let alone pulled off, during the Eighties.

"We've been playing simpler groove stuff for five years," claimed Lars when talking about 'Ain't My Bitch'. "We started with 'Enter Sandman' and 'Sad But True', before that we were still doing 10-minute jazz-fusion songs. This song is a natural extension of what we've been doing."

'Ain't My Bitch' also had the distinction of being one of the first songs from the album played live by the band once *Load* had been released. Metallica elected to play a free show at the Tower Records store parking lot in San José, California on June 4, 1996, at 3.45 pm (local time), to celebrate the release of the record. More than 8,000 Metallifans turned up to cheer on the metal stars, as they whipped through 'So What', 'Creeping Death', 'Ain't My Bitch', 'Until It Sleeps, 'Sad But True' and 'Whiplash'.

2 X 4

Co-written by Hetfield, Ulrich and Hammett, this is one of the two new songs premiered by the band at Donington in 1995, '2 X 4' (an odd title, to say the least) followed in the manner of 'Ain't My Bitch', putting the emphasis on the blues-metal style that was so much a part of Metallica's inspiration.

Indeed, it's strange to hear the band opening up an album with two tracks of such clearly retrospective material since they'd never truly explored their blues-metal roots so obviously before. Now, they were confident enough in themselves and their audience to openly bend the knee to the history of the genre they were busy redefining.

'2 X 4' has a boogie element, chugging along with a chorus that sticks in the throat, at the same time as giving vent to a full-throated roar. Its mid-paced bombast brings to mind Pantera's driving 'Walk' (whose bass line is redolent of Aerosmith's 'Walk This Way'), while the backing vocals borrow from the slightly spaced-out style of Alice In Chains, but the overall effect is definitely Metallica – and nobody else.

 ### THE HOUSE THAT JACK BUILT

Another Hetfield/Ulrich/Hammett song, 'The House That Jack Built' mixes classic Metallica crunch with a more contemporary, artistic statement. Kirk used a voice-box guitar effect to get a distinct psychedelic edge to his sound that is both unusual and starkly arresting, while Hetfield's tone is soft yet portentous.

There is a dirty, raw edge to this number that is a constant factor on *Load*. The band have deliberately tried to avoid smoothing over the rough edges this time around, perhaps aware that many felt the *Metallica* album might just have been too mechanised in its perfection. The greasiness, the stench of musicians bursting with emotion and inspiration during a late night jam session – it's all here on this song. As Lars said: "This is the new rock 'n' roll Metallica. This is what we're all about. Still heavy, very heavy, but with more of a groove."

 ### UNTIL IT SLEEPS

Co-written by Hetfield and Ulrich, this was the first single lifted from *Load*. And just as 'Enter Sandman' had given fans an insight into a renovated Metallica in 1991, so this time around 'Until It Sleeps' provided a fresh dimension that would both surprise and delight fans.

A semi-ballad, with eerie overtones accentuated by the rather surreal, quasi-religious video shot to accompany it, there is no doubt that this is the catchiest number the band have ever recorded, jumping right at you with a melodic chorus that simply won't get out of your head, and it's no surprise that this proved to be an international hit. There is a dynamic about Hetfield's slightly sinister vocal delivery that brings to mind Robert Plant. Not that the two share a similar voice, but both have a sense of the dramatic and can bring home major emotional messages with subtle inflections.

KING NOTHING

Another triple co-write, involving Hetfield, Ulrich and Hammett, 'King Nothing' has a cynical smile on its lips, playing around the perimeter of the magic circle from whence strutted 'Enter Sandman'. In fact, this is very much a second cousin – but a close second cousin – of its aforementioned predecessor, what with its chugging rhythms, strident guitar strut and Ulrich's balance between blazing bass drum hammer blows and the lighter touch of hi-hat and cymbals.

"I'm still digging what we're doing and there's a lot left to explore," stated Hetfield about what this song represents. "This is family, and it's still rocking along fucking great."

HERO OF THE DAY

Once again, Hammett was heavily involved in this song, co-writing with Hetfield and Ulrich, underscoring his increased stock in the band. As Hammett himself has said, Hetfield and Ulrich seem to be a little more at ease with the Metallica situation now, and a more receptive to ideas from the guitarist and bassist Newsted.

'Hero Of The Day' mixes a little traditional thrash attitude and attack (wherein Metallica prove that they can rough it with the very best when they're that way inclined), but it also has that element of the grey within its grooves. And at four minutes and 22 seconds, it is one of the shorter numbers on the album.

BLEEDING ME

Retaining the Hetfield/Ulrich/ Hammett writing team, the band go for the epic delivery on this one, the second longest track on *Load*, weighing in at eight minutes and 18 seconds.

'Bleeding Me' shows Metallica's capacity to build a story, allowing it to breathe at its own pace. In no sense does one get the feeling that the band are deliberately trying to stretch out the song into an epic piece for its own sake (as is so often the case with lesser

bands). Nor do Metallica seem to get bored at any point and just lose the thread. No, this is a case of the band utilising all their wiles and musical dexterity to build from a slightly distorted Hammett acoustic guitar intro and the gentle, swaying vocals from Hetfield, to a semi-roar as the band lock horns and reach towards a crescendo. But then they calm it down before musical orgasm is attained, and reach down again into the depths.

In many ways, this brings to mind Led Zeppelin. Not in the precise musical sense, but in the mastery of melodrama.

CURE

Back to the old, established Hetfield/Ulrich combination punch for this one, and it's (perhaps not too surprisingly) a return to the style that made the band so popular in the first place.

'Cure' has a wicked snarl and curling lip about it, with Hetfield letting loose with a ranting style of vocals, backed up by a blazing guitar foray from Hammett and the tightest of rhythmic combinations from Newsted and Ulrich.

Over the years there has been a certain personal friction between Ulrich and Newsted, born perhaps of the frustration felt by the latter at his tag as the 'New Boy' in town. This has, on occasion given rise to the feeling that when it came to working together there was an unacceptable level of tension, and rather than working as a partnership they were two individuals who just happen to play in the same band. Maybe this was due in part to the fact that Newsted's predecessor, the late Cliff Burton, was himself rather eccentric and individual who often left Ulrich metaphorically stranded as he went on an unexpected bass excursion that even he probably couldn't predict. Whatever, with *Load* there is an improved rapport between drummer and bassist. And 'Cure' is a fine example of how the pair seemed at last to be on the same wavelength. Listen to the way in which each fills the space left by the other. It's proof that, at last, the Ulrich/Newsted axis was indeed world class.

POOR TWISTED ME

Another Ulrich/Hetfield collaboration, this one has been directly connected to Danzig, a band featuring vocalist Glenn Danzig who, as a member of The Misfits, was a major influence on Hetfield in particular (Metallica even covered 'Last Caress'/'Green Hell' on their *...Garage Days Re-revisited* EP in 1987). And there's no doubt that the slightly bluesy style does bring to mind the sort of stuff that Danzig were doing at the time.

For Metallica, taking the blues trail was something of a departure. For the first time, the band were not afraid to show that they were more than just narrow-minded rivetheads, who never listened to anything aside from metal. Aside from the Danzig connection, 'Poor Twisted Me' also again brings Led Zeppelin to mind.

The combination of Hammett's spacey, effects-dominated performance on this song, as well as the amount of space the band give themselves within the song's strict structure to manoeuvre, makes this compelling listening. Some have directly compared this number to Led Zeppelin's 'The Wanton Song' from the *Physical Graffiti* album, and that's a well-deserved compliment.

WASTING MY HATE

Written by the power-packing trio of Hetfield, Ulrich and Hammett, this motors along, fuelled by the sort of aggression that Metallica have made their own province over the past 15 years. It's unmistakably fired up by the driving drum beat of Ulrich, a man who knows and understands how to pace a song without quickening the pulse to the point of bursting point.

Elsewhere, Hammett lets fly with some primitive lead guitar licks that provide the gloss on what is a straightforward rocker. Incidentally, at three minutes and 57 seconds, this is the shortest song on the album.

MAMA SAID

Co-written by Hetfield and Ulrich, this is one of the most intriguing and interesting tracks Metallica have ever recorded, with a distinct country flavour that is obviously the work of Hetfield, a man increasingly wearing his influences on his sleeve.

Hetfield has long had a fascination with the country music scene, but it's only here that this manifests itself on record. James has long since been instrumental in trying to broaden Metallica's musical base. It was he, for instance, who was the prime mover in bringing the influence of spaghetti western composer Ennio Morricone to bear on Metallica's vast canon of songs. Now, he has added a few countrified licks to what is an insistent ballad that nags and gnaws away.

Originally, this was titled 'Mouldy' because, according to Lars: "... it sounds like Bob Mould, it's like Sugar, it's like Hüsker Dü." And the country twang certainly adds an extra dimension. It really is Garth Brooks meets Morricone in Motörhead's bathroom. And does it work? Of course it does, thanks in no small measure to Bob Rock's incisive final mix, a sprightly balance between the hard, heavy and subtle.

 THORN WITHIN

Co-written by Lars, James and Kirk, this has an eerie pace and ambience about it. Now, if this had been on the *Metallica* album it probably would have suffered (at least to some extent) from being too tightly controlled and polished almost to the point where light would reflect off it. But here, again that word 'loose' comes to mind, as the band drive urgently forward, but seem prepared to pause for a few seconds, take a deep breath and think about what they're doing.

'Thorn Within' is the sort of track traditional Metallica fans would love, full of those thrash signatures that the band made their own years ago. But here again, it's not a retread of past glories. Hammett's guitar parts twist and turn, opening up a fresh dimension within the song. And Hetfield's vocals once more show him to be a man of diversity and distinction.

 RONNIE

Co-written by Hetfield and Ulrich, 'Ronnie' sees the band heading back towards the blues driveway on a song that brings to mind ZZ Top during the early Eighties, just prior to their *Eliminator* album.

One of the most overtly commercial numbers ever recorded by the band, 'Ronnie' has a rumbling, tumbling, chiming riff and rhythm that would not be out of place on ZZ's *El Loco* album, which might come as something of a shock, but is nonetheless true. There is a patent groove here that overshadows everything else, as Hetfield's voice dips and rises like ZZ Top leader Billy Gibbons' vocal on 'Cheap Sunglasses'.

Originally, this song was called 'Believe', changing title during the mixing stage.

 THE OUTLAW TORN

Co-written by Hetfield and Ulrich, 'The Outlaw Torn' is the longest track on this record, weighing in at an unwieldy nine minutes and 53 seconds. In truth, it is perhaps just a little too long, and is the only song on *Load* that does sound like it's being stretched just beyond its reasonable boundaries – but only just.

The song begins with a chugging guitar riff fading in through the eye of a militaristic drum tattoo. It quickly develops into a thunderous ominously mid-paced, brutally honest stomp, before Hetfield's uncontrolled sanity explodes in a vocal tirade, underpinned by a sensible, sturdy bass line from Newsted. The whole song then calms down into an almost quiet middle period, wherein Hammett's bluesy guitar effects and wails dovetail against the rhythmic pull of Ulrich and Newsted. Led Zeppelin again comes to mind before, finally, the song returns to the climactic structure of before as Hetfield leads his troops to the finishing line.

RE-LOAD

Vertigo 536 409
November 17 1997

According to James Hetfield, *Load* had shattered one of the principle edicts governing Metallica's existence – in short, 'Don't mess with a winning formula'. "There was always an unwritten law in this band," the singer confirmed in 1996. "'You can't do this... you can't do that', 'You can't cut your hair'. Now, all that's shit... just blown out the window. Everything is out in the open... and we can basically do what we want." Bandmate Kirk Hammett echoed Hetfield's thoughts: "I just remember thinking around 1994, 'Fuck it, I'm tired of this stock heavy metal image – it just doesn't work for me anymore.' I felt miserable... physically tired of it. And when you're tired of something, hopefully you'll have the guts to change."

Brave words. Yet, while *Load*'s eclectic mix of sludge-metal, skewed country music and rampant southern blues indulged its creators' need to experiment with new forms, the CD had also confused and marginalised their existing fanbase. Despite a punishing tour schedule that saw the band criss-crossing the Far East, USA and Europe throughout 1996/97, sales for *Load* were nowhere near as high as those accorded *The Black Album* – peaking at the five million mark.

Of course, Metallica's abandonment of their previously hirsute image in favour of cropped haircuts, eyeliner and large Cuban cigars may also have been a factor in *Load*'s comparatively sluggish sales. Indeed, many within the metal community had greeted their heroes' semi-glamorous transformation with abject horror. Yet, Metallica remained unrepentant: "I can't believe how much shit we got for [the image change]," Ulrich later cavilled. "[It was] like we weren't metal if we were stylish." Evidently, 'Change, not stagnation' was the band's new motto.

It came as no great surprise then, when Metallica confirmed plans to issue "the second half of *Load*" in the winter of 1997. "We wrote 27 songs for *Load*," said Lars, "and were developing a double album. Then we were offered the 'Lollapalooza' tour (in the summer of 1996). So we put out most of the songs that were done (as *Load*) and resolved to come back after a year to finish the rest of them."

For some, Metallica's decision to release two-year old material as new product smacked of little more than offering "yesterday's scraps at the dinner table". It was an opinion Ulrich was keen to counter: "I know a lot of people think it's just the scraps – but it's not. We normally stop at 12 songs when we write albums, but we knew we wanted to develop all of them, that they were all good enough." In fact, the group had entered The Plant Studios in Sausalito, California between July and October 1997 to re-engage with the material, honing arrangements, adding vocals and the occasional solo. "Two rooms mixing... other rooms tracking at the same time as we were mixing," said Lars, "[It] made *The Black Album* look like a walk in the fucking park."

Released on November 17, 1997, *Re-Load* was indeed an able companion-piece to its predecessor – sharing many of *Load*'s strengths while indulging the same telltale weaknesses. Production wise, the two CDs were indistinguishable, with Bob Rock, Hetfield and Ulrich again opting for a murky,

subterranean growl. When this approach worked, on material such as 'Fuel' and 'Where The Wild Things Are', Metallica sounded not unlike a four-headed black dog in pursuit of sport. But when the sub-sonic aspects floundered, as with 'Devil's Dance' and 'Carpe Diem Baby', the band seemed lost in a quagmire of de-tuned guitars and ponderous swamp-rock.

Again, the critics were guarded in assessing Metallica's latest incarnation. Some praised their "continued artistic growth and daring experimentalism" on tracks such as the gentrified 'Low Man's Lyric', though others (perhaps the majority), dismissed *Re-Load* as "One hour of lumpen blues riffs". As usual, James Hetfield had an appropriate response: "No rules but Metallica rules."

Housed in a suitably garish sleeve (another Andres Serrano creation, this time entitled 'Piss And Blood'), *Re-Load* debuted at numbers one and four in the US and UK charts respectively. Within three weeks, it had gone on to sell some two million copies – a figure pushed ever higher by another round of frantic touring throughout 1998. Yet, with the benefit of hindsight, *Re-Load* and its errant older brother now seem to represent a drop in Metallica's otherwise impeccable standards. Neither as brutal as Pantera's self-defining *Far Beyond Driven*, nor as innovative as Korn's *Life Is Peachy*, the *Load* series capture a band gently probing its boundaries, but still reticent to leave the family home.

FUEL
A bad-tempered anthem extolling the virtues of putting one's "pedal to the metal", 'Fuel' is by far *Re-Load's* strongest track and, as such, a fine way for Metallica to re-introduce their meaty charms to the record-buying public. Driven by a particularly unsanitary three-note riff from Kirk Hammett and Ulrich's clattering kick drums, Hetfield's vocal mantra adds necessary grease to the wheels: "Give me fuel, give me fire, give me that which I desire…"

Punctuated by numerous changes in tempo, this hymn to speed, gasoline and the pleasures of the "pumping engine" is greatly enlivened by a deft Hammett solo. Marrying the precise guitar stylings of UFO's Michael Schenker with ZZ Top's Billy Gibbons, Kirk sounds Teutonic and Texan all at once. Reaching number 31 in the UK charts when released as a single in July 1998, 'Fuel' also appeared on the soundtrack to the Hotwheels Turbo Racing game, a favourite of PlayStation addicts everywhere.

THE MEMORY REMAINS
With its talk of discoloured stars, untended mansions and "faded prima donnas", 'The Memory Remains' surely finds Metallica drawing lyrical inspiration from director Billy Wilder's 1950 film *Sunset Boulevard*. A bleak tale of a silent-era actress insanely grasping at the last vestiges of her fame, *Sunset Boulevard* is compelling yet uncomfortable viewing. That Hetfield manages to capture such artistic desolation with a few well-placed words is much to his credit.

In an inspired piece of casting, 'The Memory Remains' also features the well-worn vocal cords of Sixties singer Marianne Faithfull, best known as lover/muse to Mick Jagger of The Rolling Stones. Given Faithfull's own descent into heroin addiction, before re-establishing her career with 1979's *Broken English*, she was well placed to add a few words of her own to 'The Memory Remains'. "We needed someone charismatic, someone… weathered in every possible way," confirmed Lars Ulrich. "[In the end], I called Marianne up, and said it would mean a lot to us if she sang on our record. And she did."

Faithfull's backing vocals were subsequently recorded over a glass or two of wine in Dublin, Eire. Tellingly, it is the phrase she utters at the song's conclusion that adds a macabre twist to 'The Memory Remains': "Say 'Yes'… at least, say 'Hello'" was a line delivered by Marilyn Monroe in John Huston's 1961 anti-western, *The Misfits*. It was

also the fading actress' last film before her untimely death through a drugs overdose at the age of 36. Wheels within wheels.

The first single to escape from *Re-Load*, 'The Memory Remains' charted at number 13 in the UK in November 1997, thanks in no small part to a $400,000 promotional video featuring Metallica and Faithfull performing on a huge revolving box.

 ### DEVIL'S DANCE
In some ways 'Devil's Dance' is a poor man's 'Sad But True'. All lumbering beats and rumbling basses, the song initially invokes an air of real menace. However, aside from a psychotic guitar interlude, 'Devil's Dance' never really gathers steam, content instead to plod along on the back of Ulrich's well-intentioned pounding. Perhaps the fault here lies with the production, which sounds murky and overcast.

 ### THE UNFORGIVEN II
Lars Ulrich: "We thought 'Let's continue a story and make part two of a song we've done before'". Hence, one of *The Black Album*'s more distinguished

moments is given the sequel treatment. And though it closely follows the original track's "spaghetti western motif," 'The Unforgiven II' remains its own animal – albeit a more muscular example of the species.

Indeed, in place of the Morricone-style intricacies of 'The Unforgiven', '...Unforgiven II' conveys a sense of real emotion, with instrumental niceties superseded by a gruff, spare arrangement. This honesty of approach is also mirrored in the song's lyrics, Hetfield wearily recounting battles won, lost or simply thrown away: "What I've felt, what I've known, sick and tired, I stand alone..."

A fine tune greatly enlivened by Kirk Hammett's twanging guitar parts and Jason Newsted's asymmetrical bass line, 'The Unforgiven II' made it to number 15 in the UK when released as a single in March 1998. The song also had the honour of topping the Finnish charts.

 ### BETTER THAN YOU
The band returns to more familiar musical territory on this bog-standard rocker, penned by Hetfield and Ulrich. In fact, if one were to list the various

requirements needed to produce a Metallica song, 'Better Than You' qualifies on all fronts: festering resentment in the lyrics, a lengthy solo from Hammett and several tricky time changes to negotiate before the track grinds to a surly halt. It is perhaps for this reason – and no other – that 'Better Than You' won 'Best Metal Performance' at the 41st Grammy Awards.

SLITHER

Aside from a spirited chorus, carrying Hetfield's craven warning: "Don't go looking for snakes, you might find them...", 'Slither' is the first real disappointment culled from the *Re-Load* sessions. In his book, *Justice For All: The Truth About Metallica*, author Joel McIver describes 'Slither' as "just terrible... (replete with) a nauseatingly cheery, upbeat motif". It's hard to disagree.

CARPE DIEM BABY

Sadly, anyone hoping for respite from the last two tracks' stultifying ordinariness should avoid 'Carpe Diem Baby' at all costs. An ill-fitting blend of 'The Memory Remains' and Led Zeppelin's 'Kashmir', the track almost collapses under the weight of its own cheek. To add insult to injury, Kirk Hammett also cannibalises the majority of his riffs from 'The Memory...' in the solo section. A new low for the group.

BAD SEED

At risk of ploughing a familiar furrow, 'Bad Seed' is little better than 'Carpe Diem Baby'. Best described as a series of hackneyed blues riffs in search of a tune, '...Seed''s one redeeming feature is that it ends quickly. Only Hammett, perhaps feeling guilty for his recent indiscretions, seems interested in engaging the listener, handing in a measured, occasionally exciting solo.

WHERE THE WILD THINGS ARE

In comparison to the three tracks that precede it, 'Where The Wild Things Are' – named after the well-known children's story by Maurice Sendak – represents a little miracle, immediately reaffirming belief in Metallica's cause. Twisting and turning itself around several different tempos, 'Where The Wild Things Are' is full of novel key changes and clever wordplay, recalling 'Enter Sandman''s canny grasp of childhood traumas: "So wake up sleepy one, it's time to save the world, you're where the wild things are, toy soldiers off to war..."

If not quite in the league of 'For Whom The Bell Tolls' or 'Damage Inc.', 'Where The Wild Things Are' still represents 7-plus minutes of high musical drama: "I think we really wanted these songs to be their own entities," commented James Hetfield, "to have their own characters and I think we did pretty good at that." Mission accomplished.

PRINCE CHARMING

The blues riffs reappear on 'Prince Charming', but at least this time they're aligned to a snarling punk arrangement that breathes life into the song.

Jason Newsted sounds in particularly good form, underpinning numerous chord changes while also giving frantic chase to Ulrich's snare drum and Hammett's vicious wah wah pedal excursions.

LOW MAN'S LYRIC

As previously stated, *Load* marked a point of departure for Metallica, allowing the band to truly explore their interest in country music. On 'Low Man's Lyric', they return to that musical form, adding folk instrumentation such as fiddles and hurdy-gurdys to create some down-home authenticity. A wistful tune results, full of major/minor chord interplay and sweeping percussive fills. Hetfield's lyricism is also impressive, casting himself as a hobo railing against the sins and iniquities of the world: "I fall because I let go, the net below has rotted away..." Seedy, wizened and chock-full of regret, 'Low Man's Lyric' is a particular highlight of an album containing only moderate pleasures.

ATTITUDE

A poor cousin to 'Prince Charming', the principal charm of 'Attitude' lies in its full-on aggressive streak. Guitars bite, drums clatter and Hetfield wants to "Kill you", if only for a little while. Truthfully, the song contains little of real substance, but played loudly it might annoy the neighbours – if you feel so inclined.

FIXXXER

Sadly, given *Re-Load*'s hit or miss approach, the CD concludes with another ill-conceived attempt to create tension and excitement from a collection of second-rate guitar riffs. Hetfield's vocal performance is game enough, the singer growling key words such as "Curse", "Ritual" and "Faith" with something approaching conviction, but it's not enough to keep the song afloat. As the stereo lights fade to black, one has to ask why *Load* and *Re-Load* were not compacted together to produce one good album...

GARAGE INC.

Vertigo 538 351,
November 23 1998

Lars Ulrich: "You know, we made three pretty serious albums in a row. It was time to do something different."

Following a difficult two years in which Metallica set about radically altering both their sound and image, 1998 found the band taking solace in the pleasures of touring. In another mammoth trek, they engaged fans in Australia, Japan, Europe and America before again returning to the studio in September of that year. However, new songs were off the agenda. Instead, the group indulged themselves by playing cover versions of other bands' material. "We like to turn them into something very Metallica, different from how the original artist did them," said Ulrich. "You don't get so anal about it, and you can bang covers out in like... five minutes." Impressed with their efforts, a decision was made to release the tracks – but in an appropriately ornate package. Hence, *Garage Inc.* was born.

Best viewed as a love letter from Metallica to the acts that inspired them, *Garage Inc.* saw the San Francisco act revisiting, reissuing and realigning themselves with a sometimes glorious past. Comprised of 1984's and 1987's *Garage Days Re-visited*, numerous B-sides, one-offs and 11 new recordings, *Garage Inc.* also represented a chance to hear Metallica interpret songs

by performers as diverse as Nick Cave and Blue Öyster Cult. "[*Garage Inc.*] probably won't have the same commercial appeal as 'Nothing Else Matters'," admitted Ulrich, "but there are some people who'll get off on hearing what we do to a Thin Lizzy track."

Of course, Metallica's love of the cover version was no secret. Since their formation in 1981, the band had peppered their B-sides and concerts with anthems like Diamond Head's 'Am I Evil?' and Black Sabbath's 'Paranoid'. They had even turned their hand to punk, with The Anti-Nowhere League's expletive-ridden ode 'So What' becoming a particular live favourite. But *Garage Inc.* represented the first time fans could purchase the majority of these disparate gems on a two-CD set. "Cover versions are part of our history and the fans know that," said Ulrich. "We've just put them in a nice little package for... easy listening."

Besides the fans' obvious delight in such a well-spun package, there were also a number of performers equally delighted in seeing their songs covered – if only for financial reasons. Should *Garage Inc.* sell well, the likes of Diamond Head's Sean Harris, Mercyful Fate's King Diamond and Budgie's Burke Shelley would all find their bank accounts swell considerably.

Released on November 23, 1998, *Garage Inc.*'s sleeve saw Metallica again smeared in face paint, though this time it was axle grease rather than Max Factor, the band fully adorning themselves in mechanics' clothing for the cover shot. Also featuring a 32-page CD booklet, that contained full explanations behind Metallica's choice of cover material as well as candid photographs and other ephemera, Ulrich's promise of "a nice little package" had certainly come to fruition. However, there was the little matter of the music to contend with.

Thankfully, the band's latest recordings sounded fresh and invigorating, with

Bob Seger's 'Turn The Page' and a rambunctious take on Thin Lizzy's 'Whiskey In The Jar' both begging for single release. Indeed, the CD reproductions of *Garage Days 1984 and 1987* also throbbed with life, confirming Metallica's thrash past was underlined by some excellent musicianship. Going on to sell over five million copies (and probably set Diamond Head up for life), *Garage Inc.* acted as a fine stop-gap for the band, allowing them to take stock while determining where next to set sail.

FREE SPEECH FOR THE DUMB

Originally appearing on Discharge's 1982 debut album *Hear Nothing, See Nothing, Say Nothing*, 'Free Speech For The Dumb' is a punk anthem par excellence. Consisting of two chords cycling around a simple, rough drum beat, just six words are uttered throughout the song, but what words they are: "Free speech for the dumb... free fucking speech!" Metallica have a ball re-creating this ode to mute expression: Hetfield

roars, Ulrich and Newsted are a miracle of rhythmic economy and Hammett's solo manages to avoid anything resembling a tune. Sheer bloody pandemonium.

IT'S ELECTRIC

According to Lars Ulrich, Diamond Head were responsible for 50% of what Metallica eventually became: "We got the riffs and structures, the adventure and liberties from them." Formed in the West Midlands town of Stourbridge in 1977, Diamond Head soon found themselves at the forefront of the new wave of British heavy metal, due in no small part to their excellent debut album, 1980's *Lightning To The Nations*. However, unlike contemporaries Def Leppard and Iron Maiden who rose to rock's premier league, Diamond Head's career stalled, breaking up soon after issuing their third disc, 1983's *Canterbury*. The band has subsequently reformed several times.

Nonetheless, for Ulrich, who watched Diamond Head at work during his 1981 British heavy metal odyssey, their penchant for "the grand epic" was a crucial influence when forging Metallica's original sound.

The first of four Diamond Head covers peppered throughout *Garage Inc.*, 'It's Electric' is a cracking little tune, its lyric anticipating a level of success sadly denied the group: "I'm gonna be a rock 'n' roll star, I've gotta groove from night to day..." Metallica make the most of 'It's Electric', capturing the original's Deep Purple-like swing, while also introducing several layers of musical concrete to the arrangement. Kirk Hammett also deserves an honourable mention for an inspired solo recalling the best efforts of his original guitar teacher, San Francisco virtuoso Joe Satriani.

SABBRA CADABRA

This time, Metallica turn their attentions to the cod-satanic musings of Black Sabbath, covering one of their lesser known tunes from 1973's *Sabbath Bloody Sabbath*. A competent performance ensues, but the legendary

Birmingham quartet are a hard act to follow and both Hetfield and Hammett have difficulty in re-creating Ozzy Osbourne's banshee-like wails and Tony Iommi's lumbering guitar tones.

TURN THE PAGE

A marvellous version of Bob Seger's world-weary 1973 tale of life on the road, 'Turn The Page' is one of the more accomplished covers recorded for *Garage Inc.* Eschewing the original's genteel aspects in favour of a matte-black arrangement, Metallica make the song their own. Of course, given their insane touring schedules, Hetfield and co. were more than qualified to sing about the nightmares of post-gig exhaustion: "Later in the evening, you like awake in bed, the echoes of the amplifiers ringing in your head…"

Released as a single in November 1998, the video for 'Turn The Page' was arguably as good as the song itself. Directed by Jonas Ackerlund – responsible for camera duties on Madonna's 'Ray Of Light' and Prodigy's controversial 'Smack My Bitch Up' – the tired musician of Seger's lyric is cleverly replaced by an aging stripper. This conceit works brilliantly, with former porn star Ginger Lynn's portrayal of a pole dancer/single mother dancing her life away under an unforgiving spotlight adding new dimensions to Seger's original storyline.

DIE, DIE MY DARLING

Loved to the point of insanity by the late Cliff Burton, who drove his band mates "fucking crazy" playing their songs, New Jersey hardcore combo The Misfits were never more than a cult act. However, since leaving the band in 1987, their principal songwriter, Glenn Danzig, has forged a creditable career as a "gothic metal Elvis", who according to *Mojo*, projects "a primal, brooding presence, his sinister croon and muscle-bound frame casting a demonic shadow over proceedings".

In keeping with the above description, this Danzig-written Misfits single from 1984 is

both suitably sinister and demonic, the lyric slamming home the need for the 'Darling' of the title not just to die, but rather horribly at that: "Just shut your pretty mouth… I'll see you in hell!" Metallica use 'Die, Die My Darling''s murderous aspects as a fine springboard to again establish their punk credentials, handing in an assured and almost comedic version of the song. 'Die, Die…' was released as single in June 1999. Predictably, its subject matter gave radio programmers the jitters and thus a lack of airplay ensured it didn't chart.

LOVERMAN

The demons and devils return on this cover of Australian singer/ songwriter Nick Cave's 'Loverman', a song taken from his 1994 LP *Let Love In*. An uncomfortable melody, outlining the more obsessive aspects of human relationships, 'Loverman' was standard Nick Cave fare, but perhaps a strange tune for Metallica to attempt. After all, Cave's music was deeply idiosyncratic – one moment revelling in grandiose string arrangements, the next seemingly content to limp along on the back of a lone piano figure.

Given the continent-sized difference in their musical styles, Metallica's arrangement of 'Loverman' works, Hetfield's voice well suited to the darker aspects of the song. If there is a fault, it lies in how 'Loverman''s chorus is handled, sounding rather forced and overblown. Otherwise, the track represents a commendable effort from a band previously unknown for their love of murder balladry.

MERCYFUL FATE

As the title suggests, this track finds Metallica creating a five-song medley of Danish black-metallers Mercyful Fate's more dynamic moments. Unlike many of the bands featured on *Garage Inc.*, Mercyful Fate came to prominence at the same time as Metallica, the two groups becoming firm friends through touring together. In fact, fellow Dane Lars Ulrich felt he had much in common with them: "Very Danish guys in attitude," he told journalist David Fricke, "... very pure, very sarcastic, very friendly."

Led by guitarist Hank Shermann, Mercyful Fate were perhaps best known for the vocal gymnastics of their frontman, King Diamond –

a larger than life presence adorned in Kabuki-like face paint, clutching a microphone seemingly constructed from human bones. Like many Eighties metal bands, early promise didn't transmute into prolonged success, but Mercyful Fate's blend of diabolical lyricism and Judas Priest-approved thump gained many fans – including four young men from San Francisco. In truth, the five songs covered here – 'Satan's Fall', 'Curse Of The Pharaohs', 'A Corpse Without Soul', 'Into The Coven' and 'Evil' – come easily to Metallica, who handle the twisted time signatures, tricky guitar solos and screaming vocal lines with ease.

ASTRONOMY

Originally recorded by Blue Öyster Cult for their 1974 album, *Secret Treaties*, 'Astronomy' is a typical example of the New York band's peculiar charms. As such, the song is full of arcane lyricism and quiet melodious passages, quickly followed by a torrent of power chords. Always an acquired taste (but no worse for that) Blue Öyster Cult are perhaps best known for their sole Top 20 hit, 1976's neo-psychedelic 'Don't Fear The Reaper'.

As performed by Metallica, 'Astronomy' becomes a tad heavy-handed, losing the original's glistening qualities in favour of a standard rock arrangement. That said, Kirk Hammett's stately impersonation of Blue Öyster Cult's much-underrated guitarist, Buck Dharma, is worth investigating.

WHISKEY IN THE JAR

An old Irish traditional song, turned into a UK Top 10 hit by the peerless Thin Lizzy in early February 1973, 'Whiskey In The Jar' seems, at first, an odd song for Metallica to cover. After all, it's singularly Gaelic mixture of stuttering guitar melodies and wry melancholia are leagues away from the group's metal-friendly obsessions.

On closer inspection, however, 'Whiskey In The Jar''s story line holds all the rudiments of a classic Metallica song: a swaggering young outlaw steals the fortune of a military man only to find himself betrayed by his lover. Said outlaw then ends his life in prison, reflecting upon his youthful folly. With its themes of disloyalty, incarceration and the cruel hand of fate, 'Whiskey…''s subject matter isn't a million miles away from 'One'.

Whatever the case, Metallica's treatment of 'Whiskey In The Jar' proves immensely entertaining, with Hetfield's bawdy vocal nailing the role of the hapless anti-hero: "Me, I liked sleeping, especially in my Molly's chamber, but here I am in prison, with a ball and chain…" Released as a single in February 1999, and backed with a suitably anarchic video set in a lesbian frat house, 'Whiskey In The Jar' reached number 29 in the UK charts.

TUESDAY'S GONE

'Tuesday's Gone', a beautifully judged ballad concerning the various travails of a "Southern travellin' man" was recorded by Jacksonville's Lynyrd Skynyrd for their 1973 debut album, *Pronounced Leh-nerd Skin-nerd*. It was also the first record that James Hetfield bought.

Some two or so decades later, Hetfield shows all due reverence to the song that set him on the road to rock stardom. Assembling a mighty supporting cast that includes Alice In Chains guitarist Jerry Cantrell, Primus' bass player Les Claypool, ex-Faith No More's Jim Martin and Lynyrd Skynyrd's own Gary Rossington, Metallica's frontman sets about re-creating the vibe of the original with considerable aplomb. A fine harmonica solo from Blues Traveller's John Popper also aids Hetfield's cause, adding a folk flavour to all those twanging acoustic guitars.

N.B. This version of 'Tuesday's Gone' was performed by Metallica (and Friends) on the 'Don't Call Us, We'll Call You' US radio special, transmitted on December 18, 1997.

THE MORE I SEE

'The More I See' is another Discharge cover, this time from 1984. And like 'Free Speech For The Dumb' it is nothing if succinct in its lyrical values. In fact, the phrase "The more I see, the less I believe," makes up some 50% of the song's word count. That said, as with 'Free Speech…', there is something hypnotic about 'The More I See''s brutal sloganeering.

Again, Metallica seem to have a natural affinity with this type of material, finding no problem in carrying 'The More I See' to a sticky, saw-toothed conclusion. "I love singing the Discharge stuff," admitted James Hetfield in *Garage Inc.*'s liner notes. "You've only got three lines sung 50 times over." Probably less chance of forgetting the words, too.

HELPLESS

Disc Two of *Garage Inc.* opens with a faithful, if frantic version of Diamond Head's 'Helpless', one of the five songs Metallica recorded for their first real covers effort, 1987's *The $5.98 E.P. – Garage Days Re-Revisited*. Billed as "Not very produced", the song has a real demo feel to it, all grimy guitars and intrusive cymbal splashes. Nonetheless, this roughhouse quality suits Metallica's style, the band sounding fresh and lively. Sadly, it also reminds listeners how accomplished they were as exponents of thrash metal, a genre they had now largely moved away from in favour of other sonic textures.

THE SMALL HOURS

Garage Days Re-Revisited
'87 marked the first recorded appearance of Jason Newsted, and he's in fine form on this faithful re-creation of Holocaust's 'The Small Hours' from their 1983 live EP, *Hot Curry And Wine*. To their credit, Metallica capture much of Holocaust's Scottish take on the new wave of British heavy metal, but aside from a scary descending guitar figure which opens the track, 'The Small Hours' is one of *Garage Inc.*'s less distinguished efforts.

THE WAIT

The object of Metallica's affections here are the magnificent Killing Joke, whose 1980 song 'The Wait' is covered with great respect and no little authority. Always a difficult band to categorise, Killing Joke's blend of apocalyptic lyrical imagery and blunt-edged guitar ruled the UK's post-punk scene until 1985, when they were unfortunate enough to have a Top 20 hit with 'Love Like Blood'. Mainstream chart success seemed to de-stabilise the band, who subsequently took a prolonged sabbatical, only to return older and wiser in 1994 with the Top 30 album, *Pandemonium*.

Like much of Killing's Joke's early canon, 'The Wait' is a miracle of economy, its revolving guitar riff and lurching drum pattern virtually creating the template for the industrial movement of the late Eighties. Again, Metallica instinctively understand the band they are covering, and aside from an ill-advised attempt on Kirk Hammett's part to solo throughout the middle section, do a grand job of capturing 'The Wait''s brutal intensity.

CRASH COURSE IN BRAIN SURGERY

Despite coming close several times, Welsh power-trio Budgie never quite achieved mainstream success. Perhaps best described as a composite of Deep Purple and a jolly Black Sabbath, the band's penchant for spicing up their songs with humorous lyrics and frankly baffling instrumental passages left many confused – though they maintain a devoted, if small following.

That said, Budgie had a way of hammering home a guitar riff like few before them (and frankly, few since) and it was this quality that drew Metallica to their records. Therefore, 'Crash Course In Brain Surgery', taken from Budgie's self-tilted 1971 debut album, is treated by Metallica as one long excuse to wig out. Dropping the original's wistful passages in favour of "drunken bellowing" and extended solos, 'Crash Course...' subsequently becomes the sound of four young men thrashing a great chord sequence to death.

LAST CARESS/GREEN HELL

Another bow to The Misfits, this melding of Glenn Danzig's 'Last Caress' and 'Green Hell' provides Lars Ulrich with another opportunity to beat the living daylights out of his drum kit. In fact, Ulrich's performance on 'Green Hell' is astonishing to behold, the diminutive Scandinavian racing through the song at such speed that his band mates have trouble keeping up. Perhaps unsurprisingly, by the track's fade-out, which inexplicably segues into a quite awful version of Iron Maiden's 'Run To The Hills', Metallica sound exhausted. As previously mentioned, a live version of 'Last Caress' also appears on the group's live opus, *Live Shit! Binge And Purge*.

AM I EVIL?

'Am I Evil?' is really where it all began for Lars Ulrich. Written by vocalist Sean Harris and guitarist Brian Tatler for Diamond Head's 1980 debut album, this mini-epic of Sabbath-like flattened fifths, Van Halen-approved guitar pyrotechnics and stop/start time signatures halted Ulrich in his tracks – and subsequently put him on a plane to the UK where he met his new heroes. The rest, as they say, is history.

A consistent encore at Metallica concerts, this version of 'Am I Evil?' is taken from 1984's *Garage Days Revisited*, which comprised two cover versions originally released as B-sides to the UK single 'Creeping Death'. Unsurprisingly, the band's re-creation of the original is flawless, with the much-missed Cliff Burton and Lars deftly handling the song's numerous tempo changes, while Kirk explores Brian Tatler's complex guitar excursions. Suffice to say, Hetfield also rises to the challenge. And though his vocal range is not as expansive as that of Sean Harris, James' ability to let rip with a line such as: "My mother was a witch, she was burned alive…" cannot be questioned. As with 'Last Caress', a live version of 'Am I Evil?' appears on 1993's *Live Shit! Binge And Purge.*

BLITZKRIEG

Another song, another doff of the cap to the new wave of British heavy metal. Hailing from Wolverhampton, Blitzkrieg were briefly signed to Newcastle-based Neat Records, also home to The Tygers Of Pang Tang amongst others. This self-titled B-side to their only single 'Buried Alive' first appeared in 1981, before being exhumed by Metallica for the flip side of 1984's 'Creeping Death'.

Truthfully, like so much of the NWOBHM, 'Blitzkrieg' sounds like a speeded-up version of Judas Priest, Black Sabbath and Deep Purple, often all at once. However, Metallica hit all the right notes in the right places, and Hammett seems to be having fun coping with the ascending key changes.

BREADFAN

Released as the B-side to 1988's 'Harvester Of Sorrow', 'Breadfan' sees Metallica again turning to Budgie as a source of inspiration. Probably the Welsh band's best-known song, and something of a slow-burning biker anthem, Metallica plug into 'Breadfan''s Thrash possibilities, upping the tempo and sawing away at the subtleties – at least until the middle section, where Budgie's original minor key noodlings are curiously respected.

THE PRINCE

This cover of Diamond Head's 'The Prince' also appeared as the B-side to 'Harvester Of Sorrows' and, like 'Breadfan', seems completely bereft of anything approaching production values. As such, Newsted's bass is lost at sea and Hetfield's voice grates like sand paper, but despite these woes, a certain intensity of spirit has been captured. Crucially, 'The Prince' also allows the listener to return to a time when Kirk Hammett still played very fast, very impressive guitar solos.

STONE COLD CRAZY

As with Black Sabbath, there are attendant difficulties in covering Queen songs. For example, no matter how rambunctious his bandmates became, Freddie Mercury's vocals always found a tune amidst the chaos, giving Queen a unique grip when they turned their hand to hard rock. Equally, Brian May was a subtle guitar god, infusing his solos with both flair and taste.

Therefore, when Metallica take on Queen's most aggressive moment from 1974's *Sheer Heart Attack*, they are only partially successful in replicating its fluid qualities. Of course, in Hetfield and Hammett's hands, the guitars squeal agreeably and Ulrich and Newsted are Herculean in their rhythmic efforts, but on this recording at least, Metallica's version of 'Stone Cold Crazy' sounds lumpen when compared to the original. Live performances were another matter, with Metallica performing a particularly tense rendition of the song alongside Brian May at 1992's Freddie Mercury Tribute Concert.

SO WHAT

An expletive-ridden rant questioning the merits of casual drug taking, bestiality and under-age sex, 'So What' courted some controversy when released by the Anti-Nowhere League in 1981. The B-side of the band's punk mauling of Ralph McTell's 'Streets Of London', 10,000 copies of 'So What' were seized and later destroyed under the Obscene Publications Act. In reality, it was much fuss about nothing, the song's lyrical content no more offensive than several drunken boasts overheard in a crowded bar.

Ignoring the cries of the moral majority, Metallica's take on 'So What' is a feral treat, with Hetfield playing up the song's comic asides to perfection: "I've drunk that, I've drunk this, I've puked up on a pint of piss… So what?" As with several cover versions included on *Garage Inc.*, the band often take 'So What' out of mothballs for their live appearances.

KILLING TIME

'Killing Time' is a high-speed, combative romp that first appeared as the B-side to 'Take No Prisoners', a single released by Irish metal hopefuls

Sweet Savage, again in 1981. Following the departure of their guitarist Vivian Campbell, who later found fame with ex-Rainbow/Black Sabbath vocalist Ronnie James Dio and Def Leppard, little more was heard of Sweet Savage. Therefore, Metallica's faithful re-tread of 'Killing Time' provides a fitting epitaph for another of those NWOBHM bands who fell between the cracks of fame.

MOTORHEADACHE '95

If Diamond Head were responsible for 50% of what Metallica would become, then Motörhead were equally important in balancing the remaining percentage. Since the release of their first single, the aptly named 'White Line Fever' in 1976, Motörhead's blend of biker attitude, high-speed riffage and synapse-crunching delivery has been a staple of both the metal and punk communities. A huge influence on Metallica, both stylistically and sound-wise, the inclusion of several Motörhead songs at the end of *Garage Inc.* should come as no surprise to anyone familiar with the San Franciscan band's early obsessions.

The tracks presented here were all recorded when Metallica performed as unbilled 'special guests' at Motörhead front man Lemmy's 50th birthday bash, held at LA's Whisky Club in December 1995. Dressed in whiskers, sunglasses, and in all probability, warts, to emulate their hero, Metallica covered seven 'Head songs in all, with 'Overkill', 'Damage Case', 'Stone Dead Forever' and 'Too Late, Too Late' all now appearing on *Garage Inc.*

Given their alleged drunken state at the celebration, the group still manage to negotiate Motörhead's material ably enough – Jason Newsted's eerie re-creation of Mr. Kilminster's nerve-shredding bass guitar tone a joy to hear: "Lemmy (always) played distorted bass, fast with a pick," said Jason. "I just studied it the best I could and tried to put my own signature on there." Still, it remains strange that the one song Lemmy actually performed with Metallica that night, 'We Are The Road Crew', remains absent from *Garage Inc.*

CUNNING STUNTS

Universal 0602498702260,
December 8 1998

Given the fact that it was released two weeks before *Garage Inc.* on December 8, 1998, it seems a tad unfair not to mention *Cunning Stunts* within the pages of this book. A two-disc concert set, containing 175 minutes of live footage, group interviews, documentary and behind-the-scenes material, *Cunning Stunts* is also notable as being Metallica's first DVD-specific project.

By applying themselves to the DVD format, the group could offer a choice of viewer-controlled multiple-angle shots for certain songs. Additionally, fans could revel in a photo gallery of nearly 1,000 images taken of Metallica during their most recent tour.

Directed with some élan by Wayne Isham, *Cunning Stunts* concentrates on the band's performances in Fort Worth, Texas on May 9-10, 1997. Incorporating material from their entire career, concert highlights include an emotive take on 'Nothing Else Matters', a coruscating version of 'Master Of Puppets' and a *Kill 'Em All/Ride The Lightning* medley capturing 'No Remorse' and 'The Four Horsemen', amongst others.

Of the multiple-angle camera choices, 'For Whom The Bell Tolls' comes off best, allowing remote control enthusiasts the ability to flit between Newsted's frenzied head-spinning, Hetfield's bear-like roar, Hammett's finger-popping lead work and Ulrich's inability to stay seated on his drum stool. As James Hetfield once said: "Concerts are always fun. Visit cities... wreck 'em and leave." All in all, a worthy purchase.

S&M

Vertigo 546 797,
November 22 1999

For those anticipating more sublime pleasures, *S&M* actually stands for 'Symphony and Metallica', the CD marking the group's collaboration with the almost 100-strong San Francisco Symphony Orchestra. Recorded at the Berkeley Community Theater on April 21-22, 1999, this melding of metal and classical music was first discussed some two years earlier, when Grammy-winning composer/conductor Michael Kamen approached the band: "Kamen came to us with the idea," confirmed James Hetfield. "He'd already done work with other people like David Bowie and Eric Clapton, but he wanted to get a bit more... extreme. So he chose us."

In rock circles, Michael Kamen was a distinguished figure. During his late twenties, he provided orchestral arrangements for Pink Floyd's 1979 opus, *The Wall*, before going on to score material on their follow-up LPs, *The Final Cut* and *The Division Bell*. Indeed, more mainstream performers such as Sting and Rod Stewart often used Kamen's services. He was even nominated for an Oscar in 1992 for his work on Bryan Adam's sickly-sweet '(Everything I Do), I Do It For You', from the film *Robin Hood: Prince Of Thieves*. Thankfully Metallica, who previously collaborated with the curly-headed conductor on 1991's 'Nothing Else Matters', didn't hold this fact against him while considering his suggestion.

In truth, the idea must have been both intriguing and flattering to the band. Often lauded by critics for the intricacies of their music, it was surely an enticing prospect to imagine how songs such as 'The Thing That Should Not Be' and 'Wherever I May Roam' might benefit from string and woodwind arrangements. Equally, such a collaboration would set Metallica apart from the competition, allowing them to again lead from the front. Too good a prospect to turn down, the group bit.

Inevitably, there were all sorts of horrors to negotiate before the concerts themselves. A rock band by trade, Metallica were used to their own internal chronometers – a fact that caused havoc when 99 other musicians were involved: "There are a lot of parts in our live shows where we'd just pause... hang there, then start the riff up when it felt right," Hetfield told *Rolling Stone*. "We couldn't do that with an orchestra. We had to be 'in beat' from the first note to the last."

During rehearsals, such differences in discipline caused mild chaos, with Metallica's orchestral counterparts often starting or finishing tracks before the band knew what had happened. The problem was tackled by Kamen, who took to counting Metallica into each song.

Another aspect that created problems was the humourless approach taken by certain members of the classical ensemble: "Some were rigid and just there to do a job," said Hetfield. Others, however, embraced "the rock": "We ran up into their area whenever the urge took us, and we all got along great – until you knocked someone's music off their stand. Then they got mad."

At the centre of the storm was Michael Kamen, frantically trying to control both sides of the camp, while attaching the melodies and counter-melodies he had composed for Metallica's songs: "Sometimes [the orchestra] supported the chords or the riffs, sometimes [they] commented on the lyric or a solo line,"

enthusiasm in some circles. Indeed, the band received the Arthur M. Schott Award for Excellence. Others, however, found the whole enterprise somewhat "pretentious… just an exercise in ego". For Metallica, such reactions were inconsequential: "Walking off the stage after those two shows," said Hammett, "I really felt we'd hit a high mark, a milestone… and every time I hear strings now, it catches my ear."

Released on November 22, 1999, *S&M* brought Metallica their lowest sales in years, the CD scraping into the UK charts at number 33, only to fall into the abyss just two weeks later. An accompanying DVD was also only a moderate success. Still, as Michael Kamen (who sadly died in 2005) observed at the time, when tuxedos met with biker boots, *S&M* was always going to be "a different kind of rumble…"

he later said in *S&M*'s liner notes, "but [they] always added a voice to the song… above all making it feel and sound like [the parts] had always been there." Kamen's dedication to the cause drew great praise from all those involved: "Michael Kamen is one of the greatest musicians I've had the pleasure of working with," said Kirk Hammett. "His attitude, his whole way of going about music is so infectious… simply inspirational."

In the end, the resulting concerts captured on *S&M* were both a triumph, and at times, a catastrophe. When the symphonic approach worked, as with 'The Call Of The Ktulu', 'For Whom The Bell Tolls' and 'Bleeding Me', Metallica's music sounded magisterial, previously undeveloped melody lines escaping in all directions. Yet, when the device failed, the band became overwhelmed in a flurry of violins, trumpets and trombones, their compositions washed away in a flood of pentatonic scales.

Like Deep Purple, who attempted the self-same trick with their 1970 album, *Concerto For Group And Orchestra*, Metallica's *S&M* was received with genuine

 THE ECSTASY OF GOLD
As befitting any Metallica live performance, Ennio Morricone's 'The Ecstasy Of Gold' opens proceedings, the immortal theme from *The Good, The Bad And The Ugly* sounding both lush and magisterial in its new theatrical setting. And well it should, with a full string section of violins, cellos and basses plus various flutes, clarinets, tubas and trumpets teasing out those bittersweet melodies.

 THE CALL OF THE KTULU
Full of ascending/descending scales, myriad time shifts and a genuine air of menace, 'The Call Of The Ktulu' proves a perfect choice to introduce Metallica to the stage. The instrumental, plucked from 1984's *Ride The Lightning*, allows the group to immediately establish their own orchestral leanings – Newsted and Ulrich's rhythmic shunts underpinning Hetfield and Hammett's metronome-like guitar picking. Kamen too, exerts his authority on 'The Call Of The Ktulu', creating symphonic warfare with an army of trumpets, bassoons and timpanis. Given such a commendable approach, it is unsurprising that 'The Call…' won a Grammy for 'Best Rock Instrumental'.

MASTER OF PUPPETS

Unlike 'The Call Of The Ktulu', which benefits greatly from the full orchestral treatment, 'Master Of Puppets' sounds both raucous and jarring. While Metallica's rendition of one of their best-loved songs is faultless, Kamen's arrangement – all violin stabs and staccato horns – clashes uneasily with the relentless pace of 'Master…', giving the effect of a driver braking constantly whilst at high speed. That said, the soothing strings radiating beneath Kirk Hammett's fiery solo are an inspired touch.

OF WOLF AND MAN

The violin stabs return again for 'Of Wolf And Man', but this time they add real tension, giving the song a suitably dramatic air. Hetfield also begins to work his mojo, addressing the audience directly for the first time: "Are there any wolves out there?" Perhaps it was at this moment that esteemed film director and patron of the San Francisco Symphony Orchestra, Francis Ford Coppola, chose to leave for the safety of his Napa Valley retreat…

THE THING THAT SHOULD NOT BE

When 'The Thing That Should Not Be' first appeared on 1986's *Master Of Puppets*, it was perhaps overwhelmed by the sheer quality of material that preceded it. Here, with the addition of Kamen's influence and a regiment of diabolical-sounding strings, 'The Thing…' is granted a new lease of life.

As banks of cellos lock into Metallica's grinding riff, a group of violins take flight, circling the song like angry wasps. The effect is quite breathtaking, and amply amplified at the song's conclusion when an understated brass arrangement rises from nowhere to support Hammett's quirky guitar solo.

FUEL

Again, Metallica's penchant for speed-riffing creates real problems for Kamen and his orchestra. Instead of tucking into the melody, violins and horns end up chasing the guitars, and as a consequence, 'Fuel' sounds muddled and imprecise. Nonetheless, the track ends beautifully, with every note at the conductor's disposal spiralling into the heavens.

THE MEMORY REMAINS

Like 'The Thing That Should Not Be', 'The Memory Remains' is re-invigorated by its introduction to the symphonic process. A distinguished if sullen beast on *Re-Load*, the song now sheds its overcoat to become a real attention-seeker, a fact further underlined by 3,000 or so fans howling its chorus: "Fortune, fame, mirror vain, gone insane… but the memory remains!" This chameleon-like transformation is thanks in large part to Michael Kamen's gift as an arranger, using his string section to buttress Hetfield's vocal melody while also enhancing the cyclical aspects of the riff. And it's always a pleasure to hear the phrase "Ah, suck it" re-enforced by a dozen stinging violin stabs.

NO LEAF CLOVER

The first unreleased song to grace *S&M*, 'No Leaf Clover' adds little to Metallica's already established canon of work. Yet, its sly combination of genteel passages aligned to a rowdy, animated chorus allows Kamen to work his magic well, joining the orchestral dots to create a moody backdrop for Hetfield's uneasy lyric: "The soothing light at the end of the tunnel is just a freight train coming your way." 'No Leaf Clover' was subsequently released as a limited-edition Three-CD pack, backed with video snippets filmed at the *S&M* concert.

HERO OF THE DAY

Less effective than 'No Leaf Clover', 'Hero Of The Day''s quieter moments sound too syrupy when united with Kamen's strings. Equally, the song's slow ascent to its rousing finale seems to be dragged down by the unnecessary addition of a raft of weeping violins. Still, one cannot fault Bob Rock's production technique, which melds band and orchestra to striking effect.

DEVIL'S DANCE

One of *Re-Load*'s more insipid efforts, 'Devil's Dance' is another track that benefits from the magical touch of Michael Kamen's concert baton. Whereas the original was a rather tuneless exercise in re-creating the lumbering majesty of 'Sad But True', Kamen teases out previously hidden melodic possibilities – enhancing those flattened fifths with whirling, chromatic violin passages. This approach yields rich fruit, giving Hetfield's vocal a deep, sonorous quality it previously lacked.

BLEEDING ME

On *Load*, 'Bleeding Me' creaked under the weight of its ambitions, or as one critic would have it: "[It's] a slow-burning epic that fails to catch fire". Here, the song comes into its own, bringing disc one of *S&M* to a moody conclusion. Again, Kamen's lush string arrangements are responsible for unleashing the dormant potential in 'Bleeding Me', his use of omnipresent cellos and violins pushing Metallica into new and surprising areas of musical sensitivity.

NOTHING ELSE MATTERS

Disc Two of *S&M* begins with 'Nothing Else Matters', by far the most popular ballad Metallica have ever produced and a mainstay of their concert sets. Given the fact that Michael Kamen was also responsible for the song's original string arrangement, one might expect that nothing could go wrong. And indeed, both the San Francisco Symphony Orchestra and Metallica provide a verdant rendition of the song. However, James Hetfield's vocal proves disappointing, the singer seemingly more interested in growling his way through verses and choruses than engaging with the emotional content of the lyric. File under 'Wasted Opportunities'.

UNTIL IT SLEEPS

Much better. Thankfully, Hetfield once again connects with the task at hand, sounding bleak, indignant and angry. Kamen assists in his recovery, providing a cornucopia of brass stabs, soothing strings and outraged percussionists throughout the song. Kudos must also go to Jason Newsted for a spare, yet probing bass line that allows the string section to peek through the musical keyhole at key moments.

FOR WHOM THE BELL TOLLS

One of Metallica's more elaborate 'Grand Guignols', 'For Whom The Bell Tolls' was always ripe for the orchestral treatment. Therefore, it should come as no surprise that the version appearing on *S&M* is an absolute triumph. A scary combination of thrash metal attitude and classical virtuosity, 'For Whom The Bell Tolls' stands head and shoulders above every other track present. The reason for such high praise is that both band and orchestra allow each other space to breathe. In fact, Kamen actually withdraws his troops completely at one point, content to just sit back and watch Metallica at play. Therefore, when the strings and brass do return, they add enormous weight to the arrangement, pushing 'For Whom The Bell Tolls' onto its mad-eyed conclusion.

HUMAN

Another track making its debut on *S&M*, 'Human' undoes much of the good work underwritten by 'For Whom The Bell Tolls'. Sounding like an out-take from the *Load/Re-Load* sessions (and that in itself should speak volumes), the central riff of 'Human' is beaten into submission by a quite awful cod-oriental string arrangement, recalling the worst clichés of 'chop-socky' movies. In short, a profound disappointment.

WHEREVER I MAY ROAM

Ever a concert highlight, 'Wherever I May Roam' once again places Metallica back on track. Given the song's undeniable grandeur, Kamen's orchestrations are largely redundant here, only serving to re-emphasise the central riff and add a little sparkle to the chorus. However, the overall effect is impressive, with violins and cellos dovetailing around Hetfield and Hammett's distorted guitars like drunken fighter pilots.

THE OUTLAW TORN

Michael Kamen appears content to take a back seat on 'Outlaw Torn', reeling in those intrusive tubas and trombones in favour of muted, moody strings. This works well, permitting Hetfield to hand in his most impressive vocal on *S&M*. Hammett too, embraces the relative silence, enjoying the opportunity to take an extended, bluesy solo: "When I started playing guitar," Kirk recalled, "I was under the influence of my older brother and his album collection, which consisted of stuff like Cream, Zeppelin and Hendrix. And when I read interviews, they'd always talk about older blues people. For a while, I was just playing shuffles and boogie stuff. Heavy metal has a lot to with the blues."

SAD BUT TRUE

Like 'Nothing Else Matters', 'Sad But True' comes as something of a disappointment. Simply put, its elephantine structure just doesn't take to an orchestral setting. Instead of adding to the song's inherent menace, Kamen's strings sound weak and listless – a lightweight alternative to Metallica's otherwise uncompromising approach.

ONE

Of all the songs present on *S&M*, 'One' was the track most likely to either define or destroy Metallica's dalliance with the classical world. A watershed moment for the band, its fans and the rock world in general, any disrespect or ill treatment by orchestra or group of "metal's sacred cow" would not be tolerated. It comes as blessed relief then, that the version that appears here is an excellent interpretation of the original – full of invention and guile, yet retaining its knowing classicism.

Michael Kamen chooses to soothe and attack in equal measure, bringing gentility and sophistication to the tune's opening passages while sending in the equivalent of a violin/horn SWAT team to cope with its maniacal finale. Nor should Metallica's efforts be forgotten. Towing 100-odd virtuosos and a small forest

of sheet music behind them, the group cope admirably with such restraints, nailing every twist and turn in 'One''s seven-plus minute lifespan. As cyclists say: "It's all downhill from here…"

ENTER SANDMAN

No real surprise, this one. Again, Kamen chooses to compliment Metallica's ornery riffing with swathes of violins and brass, though the fleet-fingered string arrangement accompanying the line "Sleep with one eye open" provides ample proof of the conductor's genius. As always, the real performance at the heart of 'Enter Sandman' comes from the fans, who howl and whoop their way through the song's chorus with real gusto.

BATTERY

Instead of its usual acoustic prologue, a regiment of melancholy strings now introduces 'Battery', the last track recorded for *S&M*. Nonetheless, within seconds Metallica are up to their old tricks, bolting out the barn door at speed with Kamen and his violin section leading the chase. Unlike 'Fuel' and 'Master Of Puppets', however, this time the orchestra's intrusive brass stabs and jagged violin lines enhance rather than undermine 'Battery', pushing the song to a suitably dissonant conclusion. "Intense, complex and without compromise," said Kirk Hammett of Metallica's *S&M* experience. Given such evidence, it's hard to disagree with him.

ST. ANGER

***Vertigo 0602498653661,
June 2003***

Where to start… The circumstances
surrounding the creation of *St. Anger* are
now the stuff of music business legend
– a tale of war and want, desertion and
addiction, reconciliation, and ultimately
retribution. At times, it was also very funny
indeed.

Suffice to say, the new millennium didn't
start well for Metallica. Their troubles began
in April 2000 when the group engaged in a
very public battle with Napster, a computer
system enabling users to swap music files
free of charge via the Internet. Metallica
(accompanied by hip-hop overlord Dr.
Dre) took exception to their songs being
downloaded without payment and sued
Napster for copyright infringement: "The goal
here is clear," said an aggrieved sounding
Lars Ulrich. "To put Napster out of business."

However, the San Francisco quartet's
original claim that their material had
been "hijacked" didn't sit well with a
new breed of metalhead eager to purloin
tunes free of charge from the web. In
fact, when the band announced it would
deliver Napster a list of some 300,000
users who previously exchanged Metallica
tracks via the company's site, they were
accused of leading their own fans to
the legal slaughter. Given that Hetfield,
Ulrich and co. had essayed their way to

superstardom on the back of an extremely
anti-authoritarian stance, this new approach
smacked of corporate-style bullying.

Following a protracted court case, which
saw Lars Ulrich delivering testimony before
the Committee of the United States Senate
Judiciary, Napster were subsequently forced
to purge all previously copyrighted material
from their server: "Our beef [with Napster]
wasn't with the concept of sharing music,"
Ulrich later said. "The problem we had…
was that they never asked us or other
artists if we wanted to participate in their
business."

Of course, musicians have an innate right
to profit from their creations, and in this
respect, Metallica's case against Napster
seems only just. However, their sometimes
sanctimonious and heavy-handed approach
undoubtedly damaged the group's image
and reputation – casting them in the role
of seasoned business-men protecting
capital assets rather than reprobate metal
buccaneers eager to share their swag.

Things grew markedly worse in January
2001, when Jason Newsted chose to end
his fourteen-year association with the band:
"Due to private and personal reasons,"
Newsted confirmed, "and the (physical)
damage I have done to myself over the
years while playing the music I love, I must
step away. This has been the most difficult
decision of my life." Both Hetfield and
Ulrich were quick to throw garlands in his
wake: "On stage," said James, "Jason was
a driving force to us all. Fans and band
alike." Lars agreed: "We parted ways with
Jason with more love, more mutual respect
and more understanding of each other than
at any point in the past."

Still, rumours circulated that despite all
the public displays of affection, Hetfield
had been privately aggrieved with the time
Newsted was spending on his side-project,
the curiously titled Echobrain. Additionally,
gossip suggested Jason was tired of James'
intransigence regarding Metallica's future

musical direction, a fact that irked the more experimentally inclined bassist. Whatever the truth, Newsted's suggestion that he be replaced by Armoured Saint's Joey Vera was dismissed by his former band mates, who instead chose to utilise producer Bob Rock on bass guitar for their forthcoming recording sessions.

An injured, but still defiant Metallica set up studio-base camp in a former San Francisco army barracks christened 'The Presidio' in the spring of 2001. Yet, somewhat predictably, initial rehearsals proved terse affairs: new songs would start, lumber slowly forward and then end abruptly, band members looking exhausted by their efforts. Soon, all attempts at creativity were replaced by bouts of pointless sniping, with Kirk Hammett a reluctant referee in Hetfield and Ulrich's verbal spats. Obviously, something had to be done.

The answer, such as he was, appeared in the form of Dr. Phil Towle, a $40,000 therapist employed by Metallica to act as their very own 'Performance Enhancement Coach'. A good-natured, if anodyne presence, 'Dr. Phil' soon had the band confronting their feelings in group therapy sessions, while sticking up 'inspirational messages' around the studio. He also

asked Metallica to re-consider their working practices in favour of 'brave new worlds'. Consequently, Hetfield's former role as poet-in-residence was commuted in favour of everyone (including Dr. Phil) trying their hand at the odd rhyming couplet.

Perhaps his exposure to the therapeutic process caused a road-to-Damascus-like conversion in James Hetfield. More probably, he came to the simple conclusion that his life needed to change. Regardless of incident or cause, the group's front man announced to his colleagues that he was entering a rehabilitation centre to deal with alcoholism and other unspecified addictions. For the first time in their twenty-odd year history, Metallica were without their 'Alpha male'. For Lars Ulrich, the future was uncertain: "You know, I don't know how the fuck this is gonna play out..." All recording sessions were indefinitely postponed.

More than seven months later, a newly sober Hetfield returned to the fold. Given his recent travails, he sounded positively evangelical: "Recovery was the most difficult and challenging thing I've ever attempted – along with parenting. It's also the most grounding and gratifying gift I've ever received. The lies I've filled my body and soul with aren't needed anymore. They're not welcome." Their front man duly restored, Metallica again returned to the studio, though not to the Presidio, where their lease had long elapsed. Instead, they relocated to San Rafael's HQ complex, where sessions recommenced in May 2002.

Due to the conditions of his recovery, however, James could only work between the hours of noon and 4 p.m. He also insisted on the caveat that no recording took place without him. This meant Ulrich, Hammett and Bob Rock's creative impulses were effectively shut down the moment Hetfield exited the studio. For Lars, such restrictions railed against the very fabric of his being: "This is fucking rock 'n' roll. I don't want rules." James stood firm, and Metallica became a part-time enterprise.

Over the course of the next ten months, the band – under the continuing guidance of Dr. Phil – fashioned the songs that would make up *St. Anger*. Hetfield was impressed with what he heard: "It's come out in such a relaxed way. Before we were so... it's like we needed to feel the chaos or else it wasn't real. We'd punish ourselves by saying 'That was too easy... those lyrics came too easy. I need to struggle with those just to make them better'. I am so done with that. I know we can trust our craft and our gift from a higher power... that this stuff is the best it can be."

With a newly sober singer and eleven songs completed, there was only one more issue to face: replacing Jason Newsted. The group set about their task with some determination, auditioning a who's who of the metal world: high-profile candidates such as Scott Reeder from Kyuss, Corrosion Of Conformity's Pepper Keenan and ex-Marilyn Manson acolyte Jeordie White (AKA Twiggy Ramirez) were all put through their paces.

Yet, it was the unassuming if intense Rob Trujillo who finally landed the gig. Born on October 24, 1964 in Santa Monica,

California, Trujillo had previously earned his stripes with slippery funksters Infectious Grooves in the early Nineties, before moving on to work with Suicidal Tendencies, Alice In Chains' Jerry Cantrell and the dark lord of reality TV, Ozzy Osbourne. Given his influences (Rob numbered Seventies dance maestros Parliament among his favourite groups), some felt Trujillo an unusual choice for Metallica. But the bassist's charismatic, if crab-like onstage meanderings and a proven track record with some of rock's heavier hitters boded well for the future: "Rob makes us play better," confirmed Hetfield. "We just sound so solid." Sadly, Metallica's new bassist would not be heard on the band's latest recordings, Bob Rock's contributions felt to be in keeping with the mood Metallica wanted to purvey.

With all players now in place, and a truly challenging three years behind them, Metallica finally released *St. Anger* in June 2003. Like *Load* before it, the disc immediately divided fans – some treasuring its dense atmosphere and the confessional nature of its lyrics, others appalled by its chaotic-sounding production values. Indeed, *St. Anger* was soon nicknamed 'March Of The Dustbins', due to the frankly baffling mix accorded Lars Ulrich's drum kit. Producer Bob Rock was unrepentant: "I wanted to do something to shake up radio and the way everything else sounds." Hetfield was equally defensive: "Bob makes the big noises... extra big."

Indeed, Metallica's 'anti-production values' were lauded in certain critical circles: "Bob Rock's approach is pared back," reasoned *Uncut*. "[It's] desert dry and all-the-way live, his mix favouring bass, drums and vocals rather than the usual wall of crunching guitars. This has the effect of nudging the sound away from early influences like Black Sabbath and Venom and closer to the parched textures and knotty arrangements of math-rockers like Shellac or Slint. Unremittingly primitivist... [and] against all the odds, *St. Anger* constitutes the cutting edge of commercial, yet aggressive heavy rock in 2003." Perhaps so, but Ulrich's open snare and cymbals still reverberated like erupting kettles...

In spite of such divisions, *St. Anger* débuted at the top of the charts in 30 countries, selling over one-and-half-million copies in the US alone. For some, however, this wasn't enough. Having broken the 15 million mark with 1991's *Black Album*, Lars Ulrich – like Oliver Twist – wanted more: "In Europe, [sales] are doing really good. But [in the United States], it is what it is. We can't change that... it's a bummer. But *St. Anger* is a very challenging record [and] US rock radio programmers seem more interested in playing bands like Nickelback these days."

In some respects, Ulrich was wholly right. Despite its deficiencies – and there were many – *St. Anger* was a brave and compelling record, giving clear indication that though much time has passed, Metallica were still willing to explore the perimeters of their sound and status. By not yielding to commercial expectations and following their own disfigured muse, the band were once again at the forefront of their genre – a position that suited them: "No fancy shit," said Ulrich, "just Metallica doing what they do best... kicking your ass."

Indeed.

FRANTIC

St. Anger's opening gambit admirably sets the scene for all that's to follow: buzzing, irritated guitars, clattering metallic drums and a low rumble one can only assume is a bass line. No studio polishes here, only a dry humming, not unlike the flight of several thousand severely irritated wasps. Having sufficiently negotiated Bob Rock's latest production style, the listener is then treated to a frankly revelatory vocal performance from James Hetfield.

In the last decade, the singer had worked hard to extend his range and explore the more melodic possibilities of his voice. On 'Frantic', however, he abandons all such conceits, preferring to let fly with a howling tenor – notes are fluffed, words are chewed up too early then spat out slowly, but there's no doubting his emotional commitment. The lyrics too, hint at battles recently fought and won: "If I could have my wasted days back, would I use them to get back on track?" and the telling phrase: "My lifestyle determines my deathstyle." A song of self-flagellation, open doubt and vague redemption, 'Frantic' is a fine way for Metallica to set out their new wares at the marketplace.

ST. ANGER

And if ever a track lived up to its name...

Building upon 'Frantic''s unearthly roar, Metallica again acquaint themselves with the "music of extremity" – providing a composite of adrenalised instrumentation and aggressively inclined wordplay: "Fuck it all and no regrets... I want my anger just for me." Released as a single, 'St. Anger''s video clip was actually filmed at San Quentin State Prison, where Metallica performed a free concert for the inmates. This gig also marked Rob Trujillo's live debut with the band. He obviously did well enough, as one prisoner detached his own prosthetic leg and waved it in support. A raging hormone of a song, which won 'Best Metal Perfomance' at the 2004 Grammy awards, 'St. Anger' (single version) also featured two sterling cover versions of The Ramones' 'Now I Want To Sniff Some Glue' and their self-defining 'Cretin Hop'.

SOME KIND OF MONSTER

For those of a nervous disposition, 'Some Kind Of Monster' offers no respite from the ominous mood set by the previous two songs on *St. Anger*. The aural equivalent of slow, creeping death (pardon the pun), Hetfield lets fly with a plethora of horror-movie watchwords: "Claws", "Flesh", "Wounds" and "Screams" are all duly referenced and then disposed of in "The black that discolours us". Beneath all the lyrical purging, Ulrich, Rock and Hammett provide a suitably bleak soundtrack, guitars and drums lurching and falling everywhere.

'Some Kind Of Monster' was subsequently re-mixed and released as a limited edition EP, backed by raw live renditions of 'The Four Horsemen', 'Damage Inc.', 'Motorbreath' and 'Hit The Lights', amongst others. The song was also used as the title track of Metallica's 2004 documentary film, reviewed below.

DIRTY WINDOW

There is a hint of Led Zeppelin about this metronome-defying rock dirge. Again, James returns to the themes of addiction to infuse the lyrics with some real emotional authority ("I drink from the cup of denial"), but the accompanying music is of little real interest. That said, Ulrich's drum pattern does raise an eyebrow, oscillating as it does between clattering saucepans and robotic tap-dancing.

INVISIBLE KID

With its themes of psychological dislocation, social imperceptibility and intimations of abuse, 'Invisible Kid' is another of those Metallica songs dedicated to the shadow world of frightened children. However, unlike 'Enter Sandman', with its pantomime definitions of good and evil, '… Kid' is a more disturbing proposition – the listener feeling almost compelled to intervene in the infant's misery. The accompanying music is also disquieting, mixing odd time signatures and dissonant, ghost-like guitars. Commendable.

MY WORLD

Essentially an unsatisfying amalgam of 'Frantic' and 'St. Anger', 'My World' is partially redeemed by James Hetfield's psychotic vocal take, all bravado, grunts, whispers and screams: "We liked James' raw performances," confirmed Bob Rock, "and we didn't do what everyone does and what I've been guilty of for a long time, which is tuning vocals [via studio technology]. We just did it – boom – and that was it." The band also conducted a terrifying version of 'My World' on a free DVD accompanying initial copies of the album. Directed by Wayne Isham, this collectible piece of Metallica ephemera featured live renditions of all of St. Anger's eleven tracks.

SHOOT ME AGAIN

Another fine vocal from Hetfield drives this heaving behemoth of a song, although on this occasion, he is ably assisted by Kirk Hammett's angry guitar lacerations and Ulrich's formidable command of the slow-slow-quick-quick-hyper quick drum pattern. And despite itself, the song is also deeply tuneful, James' harmonies on the phrase "All the shots I take, what difference did I make?" recalling the intertwining melodies of Alice In Chains' now departed vocalist Layne Staley and his partner in crime, Jerry Cantrell.

SWEET AMBER

If 'Sweet Amber' were called 'St. Anger (Reprise)', listeners might not bat an eyelid. However, the melodic similarities between the two songs are, to say the least, marked. Both make use of the same descending chord pattern, and while

Ulrich does his best to differentiate their tempos, 'Sweet Amber' comes across as an underfed version of its slightly older sibling. On the upside, the lyric is tasty enough, using verbal sleight of hand to disguise its allusions to heroin addiction and beautiful, if deadly drug dealers. Hammett's sterling performance should also be mentioned. While he does not take a single solo throughout 'St. Anger', his inventive use of sound effects and sonic textures mark out fertile new directions for the guitarist to explore.

THE UNNAMED FEELING

All manner of vocal distortions, compression techniques and rhythmic games of hide and seek cannot disguise the fact that 'The Unnamed Feeling' is a very dull experience. The lyric, on the other hand, does pique the interest. With its allusions to a lack of "Soothing arms", "Down-filled worlds", "crowded rooms" and a desperate plea to "Get the fuck out of here", one might deduce 'The Unnamed Feeling' is a veiled attempt on James' part to come to terms with his rehabilitation experience. Pure conjecture, of course, but such musings do help enliven an otherwise dreadful seven minutes.

PURIFY

'Purify' marks a partial return to thrash metal values, being full of stop-start drums, bowel-loosening guitar parts and a vocal more concerned with attitude than melody to make its point. Sadly, aside from an inspired chorus that falls down the musical scale like a drunken pianist, 'Purify''s absence from *St. Anger*'s running order would be no bad thing.

ALL WITHIN MY HANDS

Like 'Purify', album closer 'All Within My Hands' reeks of old school Metallica, and as such, should excite fans who feel the band's best moments ended with 1984's *Master Of Puppets*. Sonically comparable to sleeping with an old flame, 'All Within…' is positively alive with devil-approved chord structures and seizure-inducing drumbeats. Yet, the lyric is pure re-constituted, post-therapy blues, Hetfield dragging his audience into the minefield of obsessive love: "Love is control," he growls at one point, "I'll die if I let go…" As conclusions go, this one's not bad at all.

SOME KIND OF MONSTER

Cinema Release Date: October 2004

At its best, *Some Kind Of Monster* provides a powerful, sometimes moving account into the darkened heart of the world's biggest metal act. At its worst, it validates the notion that all rock stars are in danger of being crushed by the weight of their own egos. Either way, this 175-minute film, documenting the making of *St. Anger*, remains statutory viewing – ramming its camera lens into the snout of a wounded, yet ultimately resilient beast.

Ably directed by Joe Berlinger and Bruce Sinofsky, *...Monster* captures every painful – and painfully funny – moment of *St. Anger*'s curious genesis. Group members retire or disappear into rehabilitation, only to be replaced by humourless facsimiles of their former selves. High-browed 'performance coaches' materialise before our very eyes, offering good-natured, if ultimately futile advice to a group of men, who by the looks of it, could keep a convention of psychiatrists busy for a year. Even former band-mate and professional whinger, Dave Mustaine, makes a cameo appearance, still bemoaning the fact that some 20 years on, he lacks 'closure'.

Yet despite such perception-thrashing atrocities, one cannot but feel for Metallica and their rapidly deflating bubble. In fact, when Lars Ulrich's Gandalf-like father, Torben, is dragged into the studio to make sense of the group's latest musings, the overwhelming desire to hide behind the sofa proves impossible to resist. It is with some relief then, that circumstances eventually right themselves and old faces return with familiar smiles.

An ideal companion piece to *St. Anger* itself, *Some Kind Of Monster* garnered favourable reviews when given a limited screen release in the late summer of 2004: "Whether by accident or design," reasoned *Uncut*, "both band and filmmakers have starkly illuminated the peculiar cocktail of privilege and pressure, pampering and pain at the heart of 21st century rock star mega-fame. *Some Kind Of Monster* is a hugely entertaining film which proves the line between clever and stupid is often very fine indeed."

Tragedy, triumph and a cautionary lesson to those fathers who place their daughter's ballet lessons above their work commitments, *... Monster* won 'Best Documentary Feature' at 2005's Independent Spirit Awards. It is also a DVD worth seeking out at your local Blockbuster.

DEATH MAGNETIC

Vertigo 006025 17737266,
released September 2008

"Napster. Performance coaches. Jason leaving. Rob arriving. *Some Kind Of Monster*. Rawness. Honesty. A lot happened and it happened for a reason. *But St. Anger* represented one fist, one feeling. After that, it was time to move on..." James Hetfield

As revealed in crippling detail in 2004's documentary film *Some Kind Of Monster*, making *St. Anger* had almost unmade Metallica. Born out of sustained in-fighting, petulance, therapy sessions, occasional despondency and more than a little rage, the album captured a band walking through the ashes of its own empire, desperately looking for clues on how to rebuild things from the ground up. A disturbed and disturbing record, whose uncompromising nature and baffling production values challenged even the most loyal fan, *St. Anger* drew praise, confusion and condemnation. But mostly condemnation: "I'm so beyond 'good' and 'bad'," said Lars Ulrich, when later questioned about *St. Anger*'s place in the Metallica canon. "Terminologies like that don't work for me. I know a lot of people don't think it's a good album, I appreciate that and I respect it. I also know a lot of people find it very difficult. [But] *St. Anger* had to happen: if you can't find anything musically to appreciate... at least respect *St. Anger*'s existence. We did it, we survived it and we can now talk about it in the past tense."

But not for a while, at least. As with most all Metallica records before it, the band toured the hell out *St. Anger* throughout 2003 and 2004, crossing countries, continents and more than a few oceans in an 18 month campaign that saw them play to millions at a staggering profit: "Going on the road is always fun," Hetfield once admitted, "Visit cities, wreck 'em and leave." Yet, as Metallica introduced new bassist Rob Trujillo to the perils and wonders of life on the road, they were also amassing new riffs at sound checks and in hotel rooms – each one committed to tape before being listened to again in the months to come. After a relatively quiet 2005, the following year found the band both on tour and in the studio, gradually working their way through hours of usable song ideas in an effort to sort the proverbial wheat from the chaff: "James and me went through tapes to pick out the best riffs," Ulrich confirmed. "Then we started moulding songs around that."

Though the quartet had broken with tradition when making *St. Anger* by creating material from scratch in the studio, they were now keen to return to a more tried and tested approach: "There are two separate processes," Lars told *Revolver*, "a songwriting process and a recording process. *St. Anger* was an experiment in writing and recording at the same time. But this is like what we used to do back in the day. Sit down, write a bunch of songs, then uproot, go somewhere else and record them." However, if Metallica were revisiting past methods in search of future inspiration, they were also unafraid to ponder change elsewhere. Ending a mutually beneficial association of over 15 years and five albums, the group announced that producer Bob Rock would play no part in the making of their new record: "With Bob, it was just time to kind of reinvent the wheel," said Ulrich. "It just got to the point where we just knew each other too well and we needed a different dynamic."

The man chosen to replace Bob Rock in the producer's chair was Rick Rubin. A laconic, almost Buddha-like figure, Rubin had become

justly famous for his pioneering 'less-is-more' production work with The Beastie Boys, Slayer and The Cult during the Eighties, before turning his attention to acts seeking to recapture former glories or break new ground. Hence, Johnny Cash, Neil Diamond, Red Hot Chilli Peppers and System Of A Down had all benefited from Rubin's guiding hand in the new century – their careers reignited, their music finding a wider, more receptive audience than ever before. After the critical slights and more modest sales accorded *St. Anger*, Metallica were hoping that Rick Rubin might grant them the same favours: "We approached working with Rick like a young band," Hetfield later confirmed. "[It was] 'Let's pretend we're trying to impress, like we're trying to get signed all over again'."

Inevitably, there were subtle difficulties to negotiate when addressing their new producer's style. Unlike Bob Rock, who made himself a semi-permanent presence throughout the album making process and was renowned for an almost fractal attention to detail, Rubin would spend weeks – if not months – entirely absent from view. Seemingly more content to allow Metallica to find their own level than actively micro-manage their efforts, he was only interested in hearing songs when they neared completion: "Rick's like an 'I'll show up when I'm needed' type of guy," said James. "He arrives when a song is nearly done, says 'Yeah, that's fine' or 'That might need a little bit more work'. Then its 'OK, I'll see you in a couple of months...'" For Ulrich, Rubin's positively horizontal working practices were a joy to behold, albeit a tad confusing at times: "Yeah, Rick has method in his madness, but he's the only one who knows what it is. He has a very Zen-like approach to making records."

As Rick Rubin flitted in and out of view, dispensing pearls of wisdom with each passing visit, Metallica got on with the business of whittling their 25 or so 'works in progress' down to approximately a dozen real songs. After an intense rehearsal/pre-production period spanning several months,

the group began recording in earnest during April 2007, dividing their time between California's Sound City Studios, Malibu's Shangri La Studio and their own HQ complex in San Rafael. Unlike their terse experiences of four years before, the atmosphere – though workmanlike – was also relaxed, with the comedic talents of Rob Trujillo bringing much needed levity to proceedings: "Everybody gets along now," Lars said at the time. "These days, it's fun going down to the studio. It's actually something I look forward to instead of dreading it." For more fun, and one suspects, funds, Metallica broke cover during the summer, making the odd festival and stadium appearance on the short, but sweet 'Sick Of The Studio' tour. During this period, new material was occasionally aired to crowds, though song titles were not officially confirmed: "We were trying things out," said Kirk Hammett, "gauging a response."

In real terms, Metallica themselves were not entirely sure of what the songs were to be called at this point: "God, no," confirmed James. "We had one song with the working title 'Casper' because it had been written in Casper, Wyoming." Similarly, the band were still perfecting arrangements and cannibalising material from here, there and

everywhere in the hope of building the perfect beast: "Riffs were moved around, chord structures joined together, whatever worked best," Hammett later said. When the songs finally took lasting shape Rubin came into his own, nailing down the unsubtle brutalities of Metallica's new material until May 2008, when the album was finished: "This record," Hetfield said at the time, "has been the soundtrack to our lives for two years."

As the album's release date loomed, the group also confirmed the name of their latest opus: *Death Magnetic*. "The title comes directly from one of the lyrics to a new song, 'My Apocalypse'," said James. "The power of attraction towards death was like a thread throughout the making of the album, linking things together. [It's like] rock 'n' roll martyrs. Why do they choose that road, or was it chosen for them? Why are some music genres obsessed with death? We're either afraid to talk about it or totally obsessed with it..." According to Kirk Hammett, Hetfield's particular obsession with such matters was triggered when the lead guitarist brought a photograph of Alice In Chains singer, Layne Staley, with him to the studio. A supremely

gifted yet troubled soul, Staley had struggled with drug addiction for years before it led to his premature death at the age of 34 in April, 2002: "That picture of Layne was there for a long time," Kirk later revealed, "I think it pervaded James' psyche." (Curiously, a track called 'Shine' that directly addressed Hetfield's pre-occupations didn't make the final cut of the album).

After a five-year absence of any new Metallica product, *Death Magnetic* was officially released on September 12, 2008. Immediately hailed as their best record since 1991's self-defining *The Black Album*, *Death Magnetic* found the band returning to old values in pursuit of their musical future. Unlike *St. Anger*, which had befuddled the senses with its sheet metal production style, Metallica's latest record took its cues from the best of their Eighties output, echoing a sound and time when the group were sharp, brutal and more than a little scary: "*Death Magnetic* is very cool, I have to say," confirmed Rob Trujillo. "It's the first one I've played on and I'm excited by the results. The style is really dynamic, with elements of old school Metallica, but it's also very current sounding. It sits somewhere between *Master Of Puppets* and *…Justice For All*, which is no bad thing." James Hetfield was quick to take up this theme, pointing out that *Death Magnetic* not only honoured the past, but also took full advantage of the "sense of strength" Trujillo brought to the band: "*Death Magnetic* is more diverse, like *Master Of Puppets*. Ballads, instrumentals, fast songs, slow epic songs, just lots of different feels. A new bass player, a new attitude, a whole new essence."

Critics agreed, providing Metallica with some of the best reviews of their 27-year career: "The key ingredient of *Death Magnetic*," said *Kerrang*, "is the skill with which it releases its thunder, its sense of flow, its understanding that power is nothing without control." *Uncut* were equally giving of the band's efforts: "This is not an album that reeks of midlife complacency. Metallica sound hungry, angry and ambitious again. Like all the best heavy rock albums, it suspends your disbelief, demands your attention and connects directly with your inner adolescent... Metallica are back: not with a whimper, but a very loud bang." For *Rolling Stone*, the equation was even more simple: "*Death Magnetic* is Metallica becoming Metallica again." Even Rick Rubin, whose spare production style had worked wonders in reconnecting the band with their original muse, was not above joining the chorus of approval: "*Death Magnetic*," he quipped. "Really cool album."

As journalists struggled for new verbs and adjectives with which to praise *Death Magnetic*, fans simply bought it in droves, pushing the album to number one in 28 countries. In both the UK and US, *Death Magnetic* immediately claimed the top spot, with the album selling over 490,000 copies alone in the States during its first three days of release. To aid sales, *Death Magnetic* had been issued in four different "Experiences": In addition to the straightforward 10-song, 75-minute CD version, buyers could purchase a digital download that included live shows, ringtones and a two-hour 'making of' video documentary. For those of a vinyl persuasion,

a limited edition five album release was also made available, with individual sleeves and an additional lithograph print. Finally, if one had more money than was strictly necessary and was keen to be parted from it, Metallica provided *The Box Magnetic*, a collector's dream capturing original demos, a deluxe DVD, T-shirt, back stage pass, guitar plectrums and other assorted ephemera. Of course, Metallica being Metallica, there was always some controversy to be had when it came to the subject of record sleeves. Like *The Black Album*, *Load* and *Re-Load* before it, *Death Magnetic*'s curious cover art raised more than one or two eyebrows. Designed by Turner Duckworth, the sleeve appeared to be a swirling abstract mass, leading to a dark brown, then stark white coffin shape at its centre. To some, the image appeared to be nothing more than a bird's eye view of a grave. To others, however, it was a thinly veiled portrait of a woman's vagina. Typically, the band was in no mood to provide a definitive explanation: "Well, I know the first thing I thought of when I saw it," offered Rob Trujillo, "but I think there's a certain mystique there too. *Death Magnetic* is abundant with messages. You just choose your own." Lars Ulrich, whose reputation as a lover of fine art preceded him, also proved adept at side-stepping the true nature of the image: "The great thing about art is you can interpret it any way you want," he shrugged. "If people think [the cover] looks like a pussy, well, I'm not going to say it's not... I'll just go along with it. A coffin, a pussy, life, death and all points in-between. It's all fine."

In the end, it really was. A strong, distinguished album that allowed Metallica to reassert their position as rock 'n' roll's pre-eminent "four headed black dog", *Death Magnetic* was certified platinum – or multi-platinum – in 22 countries, with the resulting tour to promote its wares again attended by millions throughout 2009 and 2010. Critical plaudits and prizes were also foisted upon the band, the record winning 'Best Recording Package' at 2009's Grammy Awards, as well as 'Best Metal Performance' for 'My Apocalypse'. Elsewhere, *Death Magnetic*

'That Was Just Your Life' is also notable for re-introducing the guitar solo to Metallica's sonic tool kit after it was all but vanquished from the likes of *Re-Load* and *St. Anger*. Obviously, Kirk Hammett had been busy storing up possible lead breaks during that period, letting fly with a fine example of the form at four minutes, fifty-two seconds into the track: "I think it goes without saying that the guitar solos [returning] were a given. There was no discussion," Hammett later confirmed. "When we started writing, it was just like, 'OK, time for a solo here. Let's go!' There was no dialogue as to whether or not we would have guitar solos on this album. They were just coming back."

THE END OF THE LINE

'The End Of The Line', or at least an early version of it, was one of the few songs débuted to audiences in advance of its appearance on *Death Magnetic*, Metallica performing the track throughout their *Escape From The Studio* tour of 2006. Then known by the title 'The Other Song', little of the original version remains present here, having been buried under an avalanche of newer guitar figures, strident tempo changes and more bad-mooded vocals from Hetfield. Not as immediately impressive as 'That Was Just Your Life', 'The End Of The Line' nevertheless illustrates what Rob Trujillo brings to the band: whether creating subterranean sounding rumbles or poking the listener in the face with intrusive, high end fills, Trujillo conducts a master class in bass guitar throughout. In fact, Rob's complete domination of the material at play is only challenged when Hammett lets fly with a frankly mad wah-wah solo that twists, turns and parries, before the guitarist appears to knock himself out by plucking too many notes at once: "Composing solos didn't jive with the feel of these songs," Kirk confirmed. "So I just said, 'Alright, I'm throwing all this stuff away and I'm just going for the jugular.' I was going to be as spontaneous as I could be in the studio."

regularly appeared in the top albums of the year listings of various magazines, taking 'Best Record Of 2008' from *Kerrang, Metal Hammer* and *Revolver,* among others. After the trials and tribulations of *St. Anger*, it appeared that Metallica had again found their place among rock's immortals: "Yes, there is justice," said James Hetfield.
Never a truer word spoken.

THAT WAS JUST YOUR LIFE

Rising ominously from the speakers on the back of a spare guitar figure before transmuting into an industrial strength example of classic thrash metal, 'That Was Just Your Life' seems specifically designed to set the template for all else to follow: Complex, jagged riffs and ill-tempered drums cut open the ears' defences, thus allowing Hetfield's rasping voice to drill itself deep into the cerebral cortex: "'That Was Just Your Life' has a great, creepy intro that sets things up just right," said James. "We were thinking about how the song might go over live." A natural set opener, 'That Was...' recalls former glories such as '(Welcome Home) Sanitarium' and 'Battery' in its quest to hurt rather than soothe. More, the song finds James Hetfield sounding angrier than he has in many a year, his sour lyrics full of images of human folly, disconnection, futility and blind men "strapped into the speeding driver's seat".

was the cause of several arguments between James Hetfield and Lars Ulrich during the making of *Death Magnetic*: "We argued a lot about that title," James laughed. "I thought it was too long, but Lars was adamant it was right. Now we just call it 'BBS'." Differences of opinion well behind them, 'BBS' has since become a staple of Metallica's live set, its militant "show your scars" backing vocal giving the crowd a chance to rant along in suitably terse fashion.

THE DAY THAT NEVER COMES

The first single to be taken from *Death Magnetic* (it reached number 19 and number 31 in the UK and US charts respectively in August 2008), 'The Day That Never Comes' is an impressive, if not especially thrilling successor to the likes of 'One' and 'Fade To Black'. Beginning with sad-eyed guitars and mournful vocals that oddly recall a sluggish rendition of Martha And The Muffins' 1980 hit 'Echo Beach', 'The Day...' soon ditches its dirge-like origins in favour of Thin Lizzy-style harmonies and bone-rattling drums. Once the transition between ballad and proper rock song is complete, Metallica loosen their constraints still further, turning up the speed, piling on the riffs and again allowing Kirk Hammett the pleasure of scuttling around his fretboard at considerable speed. "Yeah," said James, "'The Day That Never Comes' starts off as a ballad, then becomes five minutes of insanity. It's kind of like 'One'."

While never quite scaling the heights of that watershed moment, 'The Day...' still stands head and shoulders above the majority of tracks featured on either *Re-Load* or *St. Anger*, and as such, illustrates how much ground Metallica made in re-locating their inner, angry child on *Death Magnetic*: "We were playing with this fantastic new musician," said Kirk, "and the music was just landing in a different spot. No wacky doctors, no producer living and looking for every minute of the sound. We were just totally focused and totally psyched."

BROKEN, BEAT AND SCARRED

Another relentless exercise in shin-kicking musical violence, 'Broken, Beat And Scarred' has absolutely no room for subtlety, grace or sentimentality within its lyrics or tune. Instead, it seems to represent what nineteenth century German intellectual Friedrich Nietzsche referred to as "philosophising with a hammer". In fact, his philosophy of nihilism seems to provide a major source of inspiration for James Hetfield throughout 'Broken, Beat And Scarred', with the phrase "What don't kill you makes you more strong" stolen almost verbatim from Nietzsche's 1889 book, *Twilight Of The Idols*. However, Hetfield's 'rise, fall, rise again' analogies work well within the song, the Metallica frontman's wordplay ideally suited to the furious nature of the music itself.

Reaching number 32 in the *Billboard* rock chart when released as a single in the States on April 3, 2009, 'Broken, Beat And Scarred'

ALL NIGHTMARE LONG

Despite its cod-Hammer horror title, 'All Nightmare Long' is one of *Death Magnetic*'s more thrilling propositions, recalling the sheer sense of excitement Metallica were capable of stirring at the time of *Ride The Lightning* and *Master Of Puppets*. As is always the case with the best of the band's work, one remains awestruck by the endless time changes and seemingly bottomless well of guitar riffs throughout the song – and indeed, how four musicians can actually remember where the pieces all fit, let alone tackle them in unison.

Invoking the same sense of claustrophobia that pervades 'Enter Sandman' and 'The Thing That Should Not Be', 'All Nightmare Long' also finds James Hetfield returning to the writings of horror novelist H.P. Lovecraft for the odd lyrical idea or two: "It was an attempt to get back to the Lovecraft mythos... [like] 'The Call Of Ktulu'," he told *Sun Media*. "'All Nightmare Long' was about the Hounds Of Tindalos, which was another crazy mindfuck about these wolves that hunt through their nightmares and the only way you can get away from them is to stay with angels. You can't even escape through sleep."

Like five other tracks from the album, 'All Nightmare Long' was released as a single, reaching number 28 on the US *Billboard* rock chart, and somewhat unpredictably, number one in Spain during December 2008. Another track to have made a fine transition to the live stage, 'All Nightmare Long' had a bizarre promotional video that is also worthy of mention. A mockumentary style affair, slyly directed by Robert Schober, the story follows the progress of alien space worms crashing to Earth in a meteorite explosion over Tunguska, Siberia in 1908. When Russian scientists eventually discover that said worms have the power to re-animate the dead, the USSR launch them upon the USA in a bio-chemical attack, causing a zombie invasion of the States and much resultant carnage. Clever, knowing and utterly bonkers, a big-budget Hollywood remake of the video surely beckons.

 ### CYANIDE

Despite being one of Hetfield's personal favourites, and another of the tracks Metallica chose to share live with their fans well in advance of *Death Magnetic*'s release, 'Cyanide' unfortunately resembles a collection of passable guitar and bass riffs rather than a fully realised song. That said, James' sour obsessions with suicide and "death angels" granting "final bliss" (albeit it with a poisoned kiss) are among the most well-rendered lyrics on the album, the singer relishing his opportunity to again tackle the subject of mortality in all its disturbing forms.

Yet another single from *Death Magnetic*, 'Cyanide' reached number 48 in the UK and number 50 in the US when released on September 2, 2008.

 ### THE UNFORGIVEN III

With its classical piano flourishes, keening string arrangement and all pervading sense of melancholy, 'The Unforgiven III' is a natural successor to the two Metallica songs which already bear that name with some pride. Yet there

was a protracted dispute among band members during the recording process as to whether 'The Unforgiven III' would feature on *Death Magnetic* at all: "I had to fight to get that song on the record," Hetfield later remembered, "because lyrically, it meant a lot to me."

Ultimately, its inclusion proved a wise move. Boxed nicely in the running order, 'The Unforgiven III' gives a well-timed melodic lift to *Death Magnetic*, allowing the ears to partially recover from the relentless attack of 'Cyanide' and prepare themselves for the musical bloodbath soon to follow. That said, 'The Unforgiven III' is not without its own fair share of thrills, the song building from a subdued start towards a mighty crescendo and another spirited Hammett guitar excursion before falling away again on the back of a single, sustained note.

However, despite the worth of his colleagues' contributions in helping realise the emotional

impact of 'The Unforgiven III', the song firmly remains James Hetfield's baby. Full of heartfelt lines such as "How can I be lost if I've got nowhere to go?" and "How can I blame you when it's me I can't forgive?", one can only assume that Hetfield was still dealing with some serious post-therapy issues during the writing of the record.

 THE JUDAS KISS

Of all the material presented on *Death Magnetic*, 'The Judas Kiss' comes closest to marrying the visceral extremities of *Master Of Puppets* with the more scholarly approach to songwriting Metallica pursued in the late Eighties and early Nineties. As such, the track sounds like a distinguished outtake from either ... *And Justice For All* or *The Black Album*, all rhythmic shunts, Teutonic harmonies and skittering drum work. Without labouring the point, it's also genuinely pleasing to hear Kirk Hammett's return to full-on 'rock god' mode throughout *Death Magnetic*, his frequent solo flights reminding listeners of a time when the guitarist could be relied upon to 'widdle' with the best of them.

Away from the snarling wah-wah pedals and ever spiraling guitar breaks, James Hetfield again seems committed to exorcising whatever devils may have been preying on his soul, 'The Judas Kiss' almost collapsing under the weight of its abundant religious imagery: "Bow down, surrender unto me, submit infectiously, sanctify your demons into abyss." According to *Uncut*'s Stephen Dalton, some might "detect the ghostly presence of Hetfield's father, a sternly religious truck driver who abandoned his family" in the lyrics to the song, whilst others posit James is simply addressing some unknown psychic betrayal. Whatever the case or cause, Metallica's singer does not sound like a happy man on 'The Judas Kiss'.

SUICIDE & REDEMPTION

Since Metallica carved open a place among rock music's elite with the release of their multi-million selling *The Black Album* in 1991, instrumentals have been entirely absent from the band's agenda. But in the same way that *Death Magnetic* sees the return of longer, more epic structures (no track on the record comes in under five minutes), it is perhaps unsurprising that Metallica once again chose to explore the benefits of making music without accompanying words. Sadly, 'Suicide & Redemption' is no 'Orion', 'The Call Of Ktulu' or even 'To Live Is To Die'. Instead, it more resembles a long and rambling experiment in joining two riffs together that have precious little in common. At a shorter length, such experimentation might have been just about bearable, but given that 'Suicide & Redemption' lasts for a mind-numbing nine minutes and 57 seconds, the only thing really being tested here is one's patience: "Lars and I [were] always battling," James later said of making *Death Magnetic*. "I'd rather have a shorter song, say the same amount in a shorter sentence. And if an eight-minute song sounds like it's 10 minutes, then there's a problem." Perhaps on this occasion

at least, it was worth listening to Hetfield's concerns in greater detail.

MY APOCALYPSE

At risk of resorting to cliché, 'My Apocalypse' is sheer blunt force trauma, its primary purpose being to chill the blood, loosen the fillings and sear the retinas: "We wanted to end *Death Magnetic* with a bang," said Hetfield. "There's a real old school riff right in the middle of the song, pure 1983. It's a Kirk riff, like the ones he used to play in his band, Exodus. 'My Apocalypse' is like putting on old boots."

Opening like a long, lost Slayer tune (no great surprise, given Rick Rubin produced their best album, 1986's *Reign In Blood*), 'My Apocalypse' nevertheless soon carves its own territory, with Ulrich's trademark 'stop/start/speed up' approach to drumming quickly re-establishing the Metallica brand. Trujillo, too, has fun with all the haemorrhaging time signatures, locking into Lars' bass drum as Hetfield and Hammett chip away the paintwork from their guitars. For James, 'My Apocalypse' was emblematic of the group's desire to reacquaint themselves with their essence, as well as a fine advertisement for what Rick Rubin had brought to the party: "No resting on your laurels or sitting fat on the couch," he said. "Along the way we forgot some of the essential tools that make us unique and Rick helped us embrace our past."

A grand way to end a fine album, 'My Apocalypse' had its intro re-written and extended for the concert stage, with Lars Ulrich explaining "because the song felt like it could use something extra, we decided that it needed a cool intro to set the mood, so James wrote one." Aside from winning 'Best Metal Performance' at 2009's Grammy Awards, 'My Apocalypse' was also released as a single download in August 2008, achieving its highest position at number 3 in the Finnish charts where Metallica have always been treated as "giant metal gods." Quite right too.

METALLICA: THE VIDEOS, FRANÇAIS POUR UNE NUIT AND GUITAR HERO

Since Metallica released *St. Anger* in June 2003, a number of 'In Concert' and 'Best Of' DVD packages have subsequently surfaced on the market – some official product, others considerably less so. Sticking with only sanctioned items here, *Metallica: The Videos 1989-2004* brings together all the band's promotional clips from 'One' to 'Some Kind Of Monster', allowing fans to witness how time, tide and many a trip to the barbers have changed the face and hair of metal's pre-eminent noise terrorists.

Of the 20 promos on show, 'Whiskey In The Jar' still takes some beating as Metallica and a cast of beer-swilling, cigar-smoking lipstick lesbians take great pleasure in destroying the contents of a house during a debauched all-night party. Elsewhere, the Jonas Åkerlund directed video for 'Turn The Page' adds a note of poignancy to the collection, with its sad depiction of a stripper/single mother running out of options bringing a novel twist to the song's original 'life on the road' lyrics. Other honourable mentions include the still thrilling 'truck chases boy through his dreams' storyline of 'Enter Sandman', a hurdy-gurdy wielding Marianne Faithfull rasping the chorus of 'The Memory Still Remains' and a convict waving his prosthetic leg at San Quentin prison during the filming of 'St. Anger'. It is also worth noting that the bonus materials on *Metallica:*

The Videos...' include the long-deleted Lars Ulrich introduction/making of featurette for 'One' and an extended version of Chris Cunningham's well-received, if somewhat odd video for 'The Unforgiven'.

On the live DVD front, *Français Pour Une Nuit* finds Metallica at play in Nîmes, France during their 2008 *Death Magnetic* tour. Made exclusively by a French crew, the camerawork is occasionally suspect – one shot focuses endlessly on Kirk Hammett's face rather than his guitar work – but this is only a small complaint. Aside from a revealing 35-minute group interview and comical backstage footage, *Français Pour Une Nuit* captures Metallica at their blackened best, sweating and swearing their way through a two-hour set that includes the likes of 'Dyer's Eve', 'Seek And Destroy', 'Sad But True' and 'Motorbreath'. Not quite as distinguished as 1993's *Live Shit: Binge And Purge* perhaps, but certainly worth a look.

Finally, there is the matter of *Guitar Hero: Metallica*, a hugely successful version of the music video game dedicated to the band and released on March 29, 2009. Like *Guitar Hero: Aerosmith* before it, *Guitar Hero: Metallica* celebrates the life and career of the Bay Area quartet, and through the miracle of its six-string shaped controller, allows users to play along to their favourite songs, solos and drum fills. With 28 Metallica originals to choose from, plus a further 21 "songs from bands that inspired us" (including tracks by Diamond Head, Mercyful Fate and Judas Priest), the contents read like pure metal game boy heaven. Also, many contest that the downloadable version of *Death Magnetic* – which can be added to the package – is actually of superior sound quality to that of the original CD, which was heavily compressed to make it sound louder. An entertaining, albeit slight addition to the group's overall history, *Guitar Hero: Metallica* is worth investigating if only to see Rob Trujillo's hair braids swaying wildly in all their motion-captured, avatar-like glory.

Acknowledgements:
Kind thanks to Joel McIver, Torsted TV,
NTV, Blabbermouth, The Quietus, Music
Radar, *Riverfront Times, Revolver,* the BBC,
Metallica.com, Metallicaworld.co.uk and
ilikethat.com.